Is the Homosexual
My Neighbor?

Is the Homosexual My Neighbor?

Another Christian View

LETHA SCANZONI

VIRGINIA RAMEY MOLLENKOTT

HARPER & ROW, PUBLISHERS, San Francisco
Cambridge, Hagerstown, Philadelphia, New York,
London, Mexico City, São Paulo, Sydney

1817

Except where noted, all scripture quotations in this book are from *The New English Bible.* © The Delegates of the Oxford University Press and the Syndics of the Cambridge University Press, 1961, 1970. Reprinted by permission.

Scripture quotations identified as NIV are from *The New International Version.* © 1973 by the New York Bible Society International. Published by the Zondervan Corporation.

Scripture quotations identified as RSV are from the Revised Standard Version of the Bible, copyrighted 1946 and 1952 by the Division of Christian Education of the National Council of Churches of Christ in the U.S.A.

Scripture quotations identified as KJV are from the King James Version of the Bible.

First Harper & Row paperback edition published 1980.

Library of Congress Cataloging in Publication Data

Scanzoni, Letha.
  Is the homosexual my neighbor?

  Bibliography: p. 149
  Includes indexes.
  1. Homosexuality and Christianity.   I. Mollenkott, Virginia R., joint author.
II. Title.
BR115.H6S3   1978   261'.83'4157   77-20445
ISBN 0-06-067076-2

82 83 84 10 9 8 7 6 5 4

Contents

Preface

THE QUESTION that makes up the title of this book shouldn't be necessary. After all, Jesus made it clear that every person is our neighbor. And the Bible is likewise clear on what our responsibility is to our neighbor. Love.

Yet it seems that all through history, some group or another has been singled out as unworthy to be our neighbor. Some social category—which one varies according to time and place—we look down upon as less than fully human, and its members are robbed of respect, opportunity, and sometimes of life itself. We ostracize them, we assault their dignity, we tear down their pride. Because we keep them away from us and never listen to them, we never get to know them. We never really try to understand. And yet we hypocritically claim to love them.

We Christians need to learn a lot about love—and about those who need our love. The homosexual *is* our neighbor, but we haven't acted like it; instead, we hold a stereotype in our minds. Of course, we have done this also with other groups: Jews, blacks, Native American Indians, various other ethnic groups, the poor, women. We don't understand them, so we rush to condemn. We use the Bible to clobber people rather than to uplift them. Like Paul before he really came to know God through Jesus

Christ, we hurt our fellow human beings, all the while claiming that we are doing the will and work of God. But, for reasons we will explore in depth, this hurtful approach has especially governed our attitudes toward the homosexual. It is in the hope of alleviating such hurtfulness (which harms us all) that we have written this book.

We, the authors, first met in 1973, at a theological seminary where we both had been invited to speak at a symposium on women and the church. But for years before that time, we had been reading and appreciating each other's books and articles, sensing a kinship of spirit in our outlooks on life. Both of us stressed a solid integration of faith and learning, both of us were interested in ethics, and both of us were concerned for compassionate love and honest justice in a world full of hate, exploitation, and oppression.

It isn't surprising, then, that as we discussed our ideas over the years since 1973 through long and frequent letters, the notion of sharing these ideas with others began to take root in our minds. This book is one result. At first, we planned a book on general ethical principles as they applied to a number of contemporary social issues of concern to Christians: abortion, euthanasia, pornography and censorship, capital punishment, and world hunger, to name a few. We thought of homosexuality as only one chapter in this cluster of social concerns. Yet as we thought and wrote and prayed, and as we watched news media reports of the current sharp controversy over homosexuality in our society, it seemed fitting to publish our work on this subject first.

We hope that both individuals and church study groups will find in this book material to help them deal with the inevitable questions that arise on a subject so misunderstood and, consequently, perceived as so threatening. Our combined backgrounds in literature, sociology, religious studies, and human sexuality have enabled us to explore the topic in depth from many different angles. The result, we trust, is a somewhat different perspective on homosexuality than is usually offered.

LETHA SCANZONI
Bloomington, Indiana

VIRGINIA RAMEY MOLLENKOTT
Hewitt, New Jersey

1. Who Is My Neighbor?

NOT SO very long ago, the following statements were made to a national audience:

> Homosexuality is that mark of Cain, of a godless and soulless culture which is sick to the core.
>
> The teaching of the youth to appreciate the value . . . of the community, derives its strongest inner power from the truths of Christianity. . . . For this reason it will always be my special duty to safeguard the right and free development of the Christian school and the Christian fundamentals of all education.[1]

The first statement comes from a Fascist pamphlet published in Nazi Germany; the second was made by Adolph Hitler in a 1933 edict on the education of German young people. In the name of Christ and moral purity, Hitler later had persons who were suspected of homosexuality either shot without trial or exterminated in concentration camp gas chambers.

Many homosexual persons are aware of what happened to people like themselves during the Nazi period. They are also aware that during the Middle Ages, again in the name of Christ and moral purity, homosexuals were burned alive. So they are understandably concerned when they hear public cries to stamp out homosexuality. When they hear news media announcements that certain groups are, for instance, working to rescind ordinances guaranteeing homosexuals the right to live and work in the places of their choice, and doing so in the name of Christ and moral purity, they hear all that within the framework of centuries of persecution. One prominent opponent of homosexual civil rights, although occasionally admitting that some homosexuals are "warm, sensitive people,"[2] has also referred to homosexuals in general as "human garbage."[3] This opponent claims that her battle against homosexual civil rights is not *her* battle, but *God's* battle. To homosexual persons, this sounds like a throwback to Fascism, and before that, to the Inquisition. In the face of such threats, some homosexual activists have grown defiant; but others, who want only to live their lives in peace, have simply grown afraid.

During the 1977 campaign to abolish homosexual civil rights in Dade County, Florida, a Baptist minister stated that "we are facing the Devil himself in these homosexuals."[4] At the Miami Beach Convention Center, a well-known evangelist told a crowd of ninety-five hundred people that "so-called gay folks [would] just as soon kill you as look at you."[5] Not surprisingly, that sort of language stirred enormous fear, alienation, and rage. Cars in the Dade County area began to sport bumper stickers with the motto, "Kill a queer for Christ." After a two-to-one vote to rescind the ordinance guaranteeing civil rights to homosexuals, there was talk of carrying the campaign all over the country. Psychologist Hal Kooden thinks that the Dade County vote is "representative of a basic attitude [toward homosexuals] in this country."[6] Whether or not Dr. Kooden is correct in his assessment, nobody can doubt that people all over America are stirred up about the issue of homosexuality.

THE MORE MODERATE MAJORITY

It is our opinion that many Christian people take a more moderate view of the issue than the religious leaders quoted above. Many would probably agree with President Carter that they feel somewhat uninformed and puzzled about homosexuality.[7] It is true that many people are deeply disturbed by the moral implications of extending social acceptance to avowed homosexuals, fearing that such acceptance will cause a rise in the incidence of homosexuality. Yet many of the same people are also deeply disturbed at the thought of denying the civil rights of any person, knowing that when one group has been deprived of its civil rights, the rights of other groups are placed in jeopardy as well.

In other words, we believe that most thinking and compassionate Christians would not approve of the abusive language employed in the Dade County campaign, nor would they endorse the recent efforts of the so-called "American Party for Manhood" to bring back capital punishment for homosexuals. But sincere people *are* feeling tremendous conflict about whether avowed homosexuals should be permitted to teach school. And the question of whether or not to ordain known homosexuals has forced mainline Christian churches to begin study of an issue that had formerly been discussed only in whispers. We can sense the profound distress, for instance, of a Bible study group from Indianapolis in their open letter to Episcopal Bishop Paul Moore criticizing his ordination of a lesbian, Ellen Marie Barrett: "The problem with your ordination of Ellen is that it seems to set a standard that homosexuality is spiritually and morally acceptable. We feel this is a wrong standard which, if universalized, would wrongly mold the Christian conscience."[8]

The letter goes on to note "a new organization of former homosexuals" whose members claim that when they were "born again" they ceased to be homosexuals. This might at first appear to be the ideal solution for concerned and compassionate Christians in their stance toward this hotly contested issue. If homosexuality is indeed a disorder that can be cured simply by acceptance of Christ as Savior, then obviously the churches need only to preach the gospel to homosexuals and otherwise hold the line about church admittance and full social acceptance. Yet the founder of psychoanalysis, Sigmund Freud himself, did not believe that it is really feasible to change a homosexual orientation into a heterosexual one. "To undertake to convert a fully developed homosexual into a heterosexual," he wrote, "is not much more promising than to do the reverse."[9]

The matter of sexual orientation is, in fact, far more complex than many Christians realize. It is simplistic to presume that when homosexuals (erotically attracted to the same sex) become Christians, they automatically become heterosexuals (erotically attracted to the opposite sex). Some homosexual Christians may choose to become celibate and not act upon their homosexual desires, but this does not mean they have become heterosexual. Other Christians may be capable of responding to either sex to some degree (see our section on the Kinsey continuum in chapter 6) and may feel that as part of their commitment to Christ they should relinquish their past homosexual behavior and act only on their heterosexual inclinations. Still others are devoted followers of Christ and yet live in complete awareness that they are as fully homosexual now as before conversion, convinced that their homosexuality and Christian faith can be integrated according to Scripture-based ethical principles.

HOW MANY ARE AFFECTED BY HOMOSEXUALITY?

There are also far more people touched by homosexuality than many Christians think. Unlike gender or skin color, homosexual orientation can be hidden indefinitely. For that reason it is hard to say how many homosexuals there actually are. But educated estimates range anywhere from 5 to 10 percent of the population, counting only those whose desire focuses predominantly and habitually on their own sex, not those who have had only one or two passing homosexual experiences. (See chapter 6 for further discussion of the incidence of homosexual orientation). This statistic means that in a congregation of two hundred, chances are that at the very *least* ten persons have to sit through any mention of "the sin of homosexuality" outwardly pretending that it does not apply to them, but nevertheless feeling rejected and hurt inside.

In addition to the pain of these hidden homosexuals, there is the pain of their parents, many of whom either know or strongly suspect the homosexuality of their children. (One homosexual Christian recently told us how his mother wept uncontrollably when their pastor had preached that all homosexuals would be consigned to hellfire; she was heartbroken for her beloved son, and he was heartbroken for her suffering as well. Yet he had not *chosen* to be homosexual, and there was no formula by which he could relieve his mother's anguish.) So by counting the parents of homosexuals, we see that in a congregation of two hundred, the number of persons who may be directly affected by the issue of homosexuality now rises to at least thirty.

Since many homosexuals marry in order to avoid suspicion or in the hope of being "cured" by the union, we must also add the pain of their spouses, who know that something is wrong and who often blame themselves for not being attractive enough to their mates. Add to that number too those uncles, aunts, brothers, sisters, children, and friends who may suspect the secret, and you have approximately one-quarter of the congregation.

At the other end of the spectrum of feeling on this issue, in a church of two hundred people there are probably at least a few who are filled with rage or disgust at the very mention of homosexuality. The stronger the feeling of revulsion, the stronger the possibility that the person harbors deep anxiety about his or her own sexuality. That could bring the number of directly concerned individuals up to approximately sixty in a congregation of two hundred.

But to one degree or another, *everybody* senses feelings of love for persons of the same sex, both within and outside of the family unit. If fear and confusion about homosexuality is strong enough, even perfectly normal feelings may cause sensations of furtiveness and guilt. So even though homosexuals form a minority in society and a carefully *hidden* minority in most churches, the issue directly concerns us all.

A HOMOSEXUAL CHRISTIAN'S PAIN

Because many people are not aware that they know any homosexuals, and few Christians are aware that they are rubbing shoulders with homosexuals in their churches, it is worthwhile to quote at length a letter to the editors of *The Other Side*, an evangelical Christian magazine, written by a homosexual Christian in response to a recent issue on torture:

> . . . I have never read in an evangelical magazine any account of the kinds of psychological and sometimes physical suffering experienced by thousands of evangelical homosexuals.
>
> The horrible pressures against these Christians causes incredible torture in countless lives today. Most Christian gays have opted to get married in order to avoid suspicion, but after years of marriage and children they still find themselves homosexual. . . .
>
> I don't know why I'm homosexual, nor why neither prayer nor Bible reading, neither psychotherapy nor healing lines have ever "cured" me. I wish I could "come out" openly and share what I know, but the time is too early.

. . . I'm tired of seeing the gay bars filled with so many youths who once sincerely accepted Christ as Lord and Savior—only to find they hadn't become heterosexual and thus feel excluded from the body of Christ.

Less than two months ago I was told by a sincere Christian (!) counselor that it would be "better" to "repent and die," even if I had to kill myself, than to go on living and relating to others as a homosexual. (A friend of mine, told something similar by a well-intentioned priest, did just that.)

All I can do is pray that somewhere, someday, someone with compassion will begin the long, slow process of uncovery, discovery, and reconciliation of all who know Jesus Christ as Lord and Savior —both gay and straight.[10]

The letter was signed, "An Accepted/Excepted One." Could that homosexual Christian be your neighbor?

If the homosexual is my neighbor, the Bible commands that I shall not bear false witness against that person (Exod. 20:16). Thus, it is necessary to find out the truth concerning homosexuality before saying anything about the topic, since in the absence of correct information anybody might, unwittingly, bear false witness. For instance, earlier we quoted an evangelist's assertion that homosexuals are eager to kill heterosexuals; but the fact is that despite severe harassment from the public and the police, homosexual organizations such as the Gay Activist Alliance have been unswerving in their dedication to non-violent methods.[11] Perhaps the evangelist is aware of that fact, perhaps not. But either way, he has violated the commandment, "Thou shalt not bear false witness against thy neighbor."

The Bible also points out our responsibility to aid our neighbors in their livelihood, as illustrated by commandments given to ancient Israel to help one's neighbors if their animals were lost or overburdened (Exod. 23:4–5; Deut. 22:1–2). Since animals were a chief form of livelihood in that society, helping neighbors care for their animals meant assisting them in maintaining their daily sustenance. In the light of this enduring principle, if the homosexual is my neighbor, do I have any business supporting efforts to deprive him or her of the privilege of working for a living?

Zech. 8:17 specifies that none of us should allow ourselves to imagine evil in our hearts against our neighbor. Yet in the absence of accurate information about the homosexual condition, it is almost impossible to avoid distortions of our thinking. It is a universal human trait to fear what we don't understand. If the homosexual is my neighbor, I must do my best to understand what his or her life is really like, so that I will not be guilty of imagining that he or she intends evil toward myself or my loved ones and therefore of harboring ill will in return.

WHAT WE GIVE IS WHAT WE GET

The Bible has many other things to say about how we should treat our neighbor, but they are all summarized in the repeated injunction to "love your neighbor as yourself" (Lev. 19:18, RSV; Matt. 19:19, 22:39; Mark 12:31; Luke 10:27; Rom. 13:9; Gal. 5:14; James 2:8). The formula expressed in these passages is highly significant for our topic. We can love or accept our neighbor only to the degree that we are able to love and accept ourselves. True self-acceptance comes most readily through the realization that God loves and accepts us just as we are. When we begin to believe the wonderful truth that through atonement we are identified with Christ and clothed with Christ (Gal. 3:27), we can begin to look lovingly upon our neighbor. No longer tormented by inner guilt, we will no longer need scapegoats to project that guilt upon. Each time we look beyond our neighbor's fears and inadequacies, and instead affirm the light that is in every person who ever came into the world (John 1:9), we reinforce our own recognition of the light that is within ourselves.

But just as positive affirmation of others returns to bless the giver of the affirmation, so also negative judgment of others will boomerang painfully. The apostle Paul makes this point with force and clarity in Rom. 2:1 (NIV): "You, therefore, have no excuse, you who pass judgment on someone else, for at whatever point you judge the other, you are condemning yourself, because you who pass judgment do the same things." The passage immediately preceding this one (Rom. 1:18–32) ironically has been widely used as a condemnation of homosexual love. But Paul's words about homosexual acts must be read within their context, as indeed every passage of Scripture must be read. Paul's "therefore" in the very next verse (Rom. 2:1, quoted above) bases his warning against condemning others precisely on the very passage that has been used to condemn homosexuals! Although interrupted by a chapter division, the flow of thought runs with tight logic from Rom. 1:18 through Rom. 2:16.

This passage explains why deeply homophobic people—that is, people who are enraged and feel revulsion toward homosexuality—need our help just as much as homosexuals themselves. Because of human feelings of guilt and alienation, we have a tendency to latch on to certain passages of Scripture in order to condemn others, in an attempt to distance ourselves from our own guilty feelings. But by so doing, we only increase the sense of condemnation we are laboring under. As we will see in chapter 5, Rom. 1:18–32 is a passage primarily concerning idolatry, specifying that worship of the body and worship of things, indecent sexual acts and such sins as envy, gossip, heartlessness, and slander all grow out of the stubborn refusal to recognize the invisible qualities of God through the visible creation. Paul is pointing out that *every* human being has been guilty to one degree or another of such alienation from God. It is one of the most dreadful ironies of Christendom that instead of responding to the utter *universality* of Paul's remarks in chapter 1 of Romans, many Christians have tried to evade confrontation with their own idolatrous ways by applying the whole passage only to homosexuals! By such scapegoating, these Christians have placed themselves directly under the self-condemnation described in Rom. 2:1: "At whatever point you judge the other, you are condemning yourself." Condemnation is, indeed, a boomerang. Fortunately, so is loving acceptance. Whatever we do to our neighbor, for good or evil, we do to ourselves.

WHERE I FIND NEED, I FIND MY NEIGHBOR

But who *is* my neighbor? We must remind ourselves that when a certain expert in Jewish law was testing Christ and trying to justify himself, he asked Christ that very same question. In answer, Jesus told him the story of the man who was beaten by thieves and left for dead. A priest saw the man's plight, and later a Levite, but both chose to remain uninvolved. Finally, a Samaritan took pity on the man and, at great personal inconvenience and expense, helped him to safety. Jesus put it to the lawyer: Which one of these was the neighbor to the unfortunate man? The lawyer naturally had no choice except to acknowledge that the Samaritan, who had shown mercy, was the real neighbor. Jesus said to the lawyer, "Go, and do as he did" (Luke 10:37).

It is interesting that Jesus did not define the concept of "neighbor" by geographical closeness, nor by race, nor by religion, but only by *need.* Anyone who crosses my path and needs my help is my neighbor. And I am neighbor to anyone to whom I give assistance. As Jesus said to the lawyer about loving God and neighbor with all his soul and strength and mind, *"Do that and you will live"* (Luke 10:28). For when the sheep are separated from the goats in the day of judgment, the king will say to those on his right hand, "Anything you did for one of my brothers here, however humble, you did for me" (Matt. 25:40).

In the light of Christ's pronouncements on neighborliness, let us pause to ask ourselves some questions.

Do I care about the need of homosexuals who are without Christ and who cannot respond to an invitation based on the condition that they must either become heterosexual or live celibate forever after?

Do I care about the need of hidden homosexual Christians whose self-acceptance is impeded by the well-meaning remarks of those who have not taken the trouble to understand the homosexual condition?

Do I care about the need of self-confessed homosexual Christians who endure rejection from those who make them into scapegoats for their own inner alienation?

Do I care about the need of the parents of homosexuals who endure agonies of guilt and humiliation, wondering what they did wrong?

Do I care about the need of the bewildered spouses and children of homosexuals who married out of a desire to hide, disprove, or "cure" their homosexuality?

Do I care about the need of those who must storm and rage against homosexuals because they are afraid about their own sexuality?

Do I care about the need of Christian communities to build healthy, responsible attitudes toward human sexuality in all its tremendous variety?

Do I care enough to do something constructive about homosexuality, such as informing myself so that I can inform others?

If your answer to any of the above questions is yes, then this book is written for you.

❧ 2. The Risks and Challenges of Moral Growth

IT IS natural to feel a certain amount of fear when reopening questions that have seemed to be as closed as the topic of homosexuality has been to church people for many years. But the wider truth is that *any* questioning of familiar ethical standards on any topic, no matter how localized, can feel frightening to a person who sincerely wants to live a godly life.

The difference between moral maturity and moral childishness has nothing to do with puberty or chronological age. The morally mature person is one who has not only sorted through the standards learned in childhood, rejecting those that no longer apply, and accepting and internalizing those that still do apply. He or she is also one who has developed the courage to obey God's voice in those highly unusual situations when long-accepted standards must for some reason be transcended. Rising above standards that have been ingrained from childhood may involve tremendous struggle and often real terror. But the refusal even to consider the possibility of such transcendence may well lead to moral rigor mortis. In order to deepen our grasp of the necessity for moral maturity, we'd like to focus now on two stories, one biblical and one extra-biblical, with a third story to follow later.

THE AGONY OF OUTGROWING FAMILIAR PATTERNS

Our first narrative, recorded in Acts, chapters 10 and 11, involves Simon Peter, the Lord's most impetuous disciple. One day Peter went for prayer to the roof of the house where he was staying. After saying his prayers and while hungrily awaiting dinner, Peter experienced an extremely unsettling vision. He saw a great sheet-like container full of wild animals and other four-footed beasts, birds of the air, and creeping things descend from heaven. And he heard a voice say: "Get up, Peter. Kill and eat." Peter's flesh must have crawled at the very suggestion that he violate the dietary laws he had been taught from childhood: "All creatures that teem on the ground, crawl on their bellies . . . you shall not eat, because they are vermin which contaminate. . . . you shall make yourselves holy and keep yourselves holy, because I am holy. You shall not defile yourselves with any teeming creature that creeps on the ground" (Lev. 11:42–44).

Knowing that the voice that he heard was that of the Lord, Peter must have quickly considered the available possibilities. Perhaps there were some animals in the sheet that chewed the cud and had divided hoofs and were therefore permissible for Jews to eat. Could he manage to separate one of those from the rest? But no, the presence of so many unclean creatures made his gorge rise. And there was no way on this roof top to kill the animal or prepare the flesh in a kosher manner. Peter's answer was certain: "No, Lord, no: I have never eaten anything profane or unclean."

Again that voice: "It is not for you to call profane what God counts clean." And then the whole sequence was repeated: the command to kill and eat, Peter's revulsion based on careful training in Jewish dietary laws, his refusal, and the Lord's correction of Peter's concept of cleanness. What could this mean? Certainly God Himself had given the dietary laws to His people the Israelites (Lev. 11, Deut. 14). They were God's Word. Yet this was God's own voice, giving instructions to transgress that general law in this specific case! A third time the whole sequence occurred. Again Peter refused to obey God's voice. He simply *could not* transcend rules he had followed for so long and with such care. Not even in response to the voice of the Lord!

After the vision had passed, Peter sat thinking about it. Maybe he remembered a time when he'd been given three opportunities to show his loyalty to the Lord and had failed all three (Matt. 26:33–35, 69–75). While he was still wrapped in thought, God's Spirit told him that some men were looking for him and that he should not fear to go with them because they had been sent by God. Peter must have wondered why God had bothered to tell him not to fear a couple of strangers. After all, he did not consider himself a coward. But when he heard where the men came from—the house of a prominent Gentile—he understood instantly. He normally would have recoiled from any association with such persons, as he had been fully trained in Jewish laws that prohibited associating with Gentiles or visiting in their houses (Acts 10:28; Josh. 23:7). But this time, the *fourth* opportunity, Peter knew better than to disobey the voice of God. Without hesitation, he invited the men into the house and the next day went with them to preach the gospel to the Gentiles.

For Peter, such moral growth was not easy. It involved him in conflict with circumcised Christians in Jerusalem who at first could not understand why Peter had violated Jewish law. Later, Peter (also called Cephas) would give in to Jewish-Christian pressure and separate himself from the Gentiles to such a degree that Paul had to correct him in public (Gal. 2:11–16). But for now, because Peter had directly experienced the power of God's Spirit in his dealings with the Gentiles, he was able to explain his actions to the satisfaction of his fellow believers. Confronted with the evidence that God was working in new and unexpected ways, the Jewish Christians were "astonished that the gift of the Holy Spirit should have been poured out even on Gentiles" (Acts 10:45, 11:18). *Even on Gentiles.* It was mind-boggling. But the strength of Peter's vision and the overt manifestations of the Spirit forced them to develop a more mature understanding of the workings of God.

GOD'S VOICE, OR SOCIETY'S VOICE?

Our second story comes from one of the most justly famous of American novels, Mark Twain's *Huckleberry Finn.* Huck, who has been raised to believe in the sacredness of private property (even if that property happens to be a human being) is appalled when he confronts the moral implications of helping his black friend, Jim, escape from slavery. At one point, when Jim has been captured and is imprisoned on the Phelps farm, Huck feels God is warning him to desist from such evil ways:

> It hit me all of a sudden that here was the plain hand of Providence slapping me in the face and letting me know my wickedness was being watched all the time up there in heaven, whilst I was stealing a poor old woman's nigger, that hadn't ever done me no harm, and now was showing me there's One that's always on the lookout, and ain't a-going to allow no such miserable doings to go only just so fur and no further, I most dropped in my tracks I was so scared.[1]

To Huck, as to every morally immature person, the voice of socialization seems to be the voice of God. Huck decides to pray; but his socially conditioned conscience tells him that God will not hear his prayer until he has written to Miss Watson, Jim's slaveowner, telling her how to recover her "property." He writes the note and at first feels "all washed clean of sin for the first time I had ever felt so in my life." He assumes that by upholding the laws of private property and returning a human being to slavery, he has saved himself from hell. But then he begins to think about Jim: "And got to thinking over our trip down the river; and I see Jim before me all the time in the day and in the night-time, sometimes moonlight, sometimes storms, and we a-floating along, talking and singing and laughing. But somehow I couldn't seem to strike no places to harden me against him, but only the other kind." Huck remembers Jim's humanity, his warmth, his kindness, and his grateful dependence on Huck as his only friend in the world. And suddenly, Huck tears up the note, saying, "All right, then, I'll go to hell,"[2] and resolves to steal Jim from the Phelps farm, regardless of the penalty.

Did Huck choose to serve humanity rather than God? Was his willingness to go to hell in order to free a friend from slavery simply a matter of blasphemous secularism? Before we jump to that conclusion, we might be wise to remind ourselves that the apostle Paul, recognizing that some of his Jewish kinsmen were not among God's elect "children of promise," declared that he could wish himself accursed on their behalf (Rom. 9:3). In other words, Paul would have been willing to go to hell himself if that would have changed the destiny of his Jewish friends. Similarly, Huck was willing to take any risks necessary to help Jim. "No one has greater love," said Jesus, "than the one who lays down his life for his friends" (John 15:13, NIV).

In both of our stories we see a human being struggling for the courage to transcend what he believes to be a divinely ordained rule. Admittedly, there are some important distinctions between them. Peter had to contend with his knowledge of Jewish law as recorded in Holy Scripture. He had to have the courage to listen to the voice of God speaking to him directly, and had to obey that voice even when it ordered him to do something counter to the laws that the same voice had earlier delivered to the children of Israel.

In Huck Finn's case, there was no question of an individual voice, recognizable as God's, directing him to disobey a more general God-given law. For Huck, it wasn't that clear-cut. Huck had been taught that private property was sacred, that to interfere with someone else's possession was to incur the wrath of God. Where Huck grew up, slavery was not considered immoral, but stealing was. Biblical injunctions against stealing were invoked frequently, since they protected the rich and powerful and helped to control the poor and needy. But nobody looked past the most literal sense of New Testament references to slavery. Nobody paid any attention to the liberating principles of passages like Gal. 3:28 and Col. 3:11. Since slavery had been part of first-century society, it was assumed that slavery was forever a part of God's plan for the human race. Huck had never questioned that this assumption was God's truth for his time and for all time. The only voice that encouraged him to help Jim was the still small voice of his own compassion. Because of his training, Huck assumed that his most decent human impulses were evil. But that did not *make* them evil. "Even if our conscience condemns us," says John, "God is greater than our conscience and knows all" (1 John 3:20).

CAN WE EVADE STRUGGLE?

Each of our stories emphasizes an important point about moral and ethical choice. Peter's story indicates that there are times when human beings are directed to transcend general laws of God and society because of the specific work God has chosen them to do. Gone is the certainty of assuming that all we need to do is simply cling to the rules handed down to us by decent people. Gone, even, is the simplistic use of Scripture. Had Peter simply continued to obey the command of Josh. 23:7 that Jews should not associate with Gentiles, then he would not have had the privilege of carrying the gospel to Cornelius and his household. Although the biblical rule had been a perfectly good one, intended to keep the Jews from slipping into idolatrous ways, Peter was made to recognize that in his situation it no longer applied, and that he should obey instead the directions given to him personally by God's voice. Attention to this story warns us that thoughtless obedience, even to a passage of Scripture, can be disastrous in its effects on our moral life.

Huck's story demonstrates how dangerously easy it is to confuse the voice of society with the voice of God. It warns us against the too-easy assumption that our consciences will always give us correct guidance. Having been brought up in a slave-owning society, Huck felt it natural to classify human beings as property if they had been paid for legally. It was easy to find moral justification for slavery in a few biblical passages if they were interpreted on the most literalistic level and without attention to context. Take, for instance, 1 Peter 2:18 (NIV): "Slaves, submit yourselves to your masters with all respect." What could be clearer than that? To help a slave escape was to violate the obvious, clear meaning of the Word of God. Anyone who said that a more careful exegesis would unearth the liberating principle of the One Body of Christ, with all Christians submitting to and caring for each other, and thus would do away with the concept of slavery, was accused of twisting Scripture in order to evade what was obviously there on the surface. In such a society, poor Huckleberry was left with no choice except to think that his decent human concern was contrary to God's revealed will and therefore was an evil for which he would be punished in hell.

Thinking that he was violating the will of God, Huck chose human liberation. But what he was *really* violating were the standards of a corrupt society. Those standards had been programed into his conscience, so that his heart condemned him even when God did not. His dilemma illustrates the fact that we sometimes feel very afraid to do what we sense to be right, not because we would actually be violating the will of God, but because we have been programed in such a way that we think the voice of a corrupt society *is* the will of God. For instance, in recent years many married persons have felt that, as human beings who are equally God's image bearers, they should rightfully relate to each other as equals. But all around them the voice of society says, as it has said for centuries, that it is proper for the woman to play only a secondary and supportive role. It has been only too easy for many churches to support society's sinful assumptions by latching on to a few verses of Scripture interpreted literalistically and without attention to context.

Anyone who tries to interpret the Bible contextually on this point, showing that mutual submission is everywhere applied to Christians married to each other and to all other Christians,[3] is accused of twisting the Scripture in order to evade what is obviously there on the surface. The result is that some Christian married couples have chosen to live in mutual submission of the husband to the wife and the wife to the husband, yet have staggered under the burden of feeling they were violating the will of God. In fact they were violating only the assumptions of a fallen society as those assumptions have been rationalized by a superficial reading of the Bible. Other couples have struggled along in an unequal partnership, the woman oppressed by her subjection and the man oppressed by his role as oppressor, in the delusion that this was God's requirement for them both. It is as if Huck had chosen to save his own soul by allowing Jim to be returned to slavery. It is as if Peter had chosen to obey Jewish law by clinging to Josh. 23:7 and letting the Gentiles do without the gospel.

THE SELF-EXAMINED LIFE

Both stories challenge us to study the Bible more closely. If we are to seek scriptural guidance concerning our moral and ethical attitudes, we must be extremely careful in our interpretations. When we assume that the Bible is perfectly clear on a moral issue—so clear that only a fool or a dishonest person could possibly differ from our view of things—that overconfidence should alert us to the possibility that our egos are clouding our interpretations. Self-suspicion is especially in order when our view happens to coincide with the prevailing view, whether of a particular church or the secular society. If and when such a correlation is present, we cannot reasonably doubt that we need to open our minds to careful reconsideration.

Perhaps, after full and honest examination of all available evidence, we will still arrive at the same conclusions—but in the process, we will have internalized the issue and thus will have matured at least as far as that issue is concerned. But perhaps we will be forced to move beyond the comfortable certainty of an old, familiar rule. As G.C. Berkouwer says: "To confess Holy Scripture and its authority is to be aware of the command to understand and to interpret it. It always places us at the beginning of a road that we can only travel in 'fear and trepidation'."[4]

Those who stick to the thoughtless repetition of selected proof texts in order to rationalize a comfortable alliance with society's standards frequently fling accusations at those who want to probe the depths of the Bible. "By introducing such questions you will destroy the Bible's authority over humanity," they say. Or, "You will undermine belief in biblical infallibility." The painful irony here is that those who refuse to search the Scriptures concerning the assumptions of society are the ones who are refusing to submit social customs to the judgment of the Bible. By that refusal they are helping to erode biblical authority in contemporary society. Not the seekers, but those who fear to seek, are those who doubt biblical infallibility.

Here again we agree with Berkouwer, who comments that "those who, because of hesitancy and wariness, abandon new hermeneutical questions contribute to the relativising of scriptural authority. . . . In the history of the church it is evident that unrest can never be removed by ecclesiastical inattention to real questions."[5] We need the courage and faith to face the challenges posed by the questions of our day. And the Holy Spirit can supply the courage and faith we need, for as Luther said, "The Holy Spirit is no skeptic."[6] We can probe, question, and study fearlessly, confident that the Bible is adequate to any honest dialogue.

THE PERIL OF MISGUIDED CHOICE

But what of the personal risks involved in moving beyond thoughtless adherence to general laws and rules? Granted that Peter and Huck were ultimately right about their decisions. But doesn't their example give the perhaps misleading impression that simply listening to an inner voice is a safer moral guide than obeying the Bible's guidelines and society's well-established rules? And doesn't such an attitude contain perilous possibilities? It is bad enough to confuse the voice of *society* with the will of God. Isn't it even worse to confuse our own *subjective desires* with the will of God?

Here again, the Bible supplies us with an enlightening story, that of Samson recorded in Judges, chapters 13–16. Although Samson is listed among the great heroes of faith in Hebrews, chapter 11, the extreme violence of his personality causes great difficulty for many contemporary Christians. But we do not intend to focus our thinking on that aspect of the Samson story. Rather, we want to focus on Samson's method of finding the will of God for his life.

When Samson chose to marry the woman at Timnath, a Philistine, he made that decision not simply on the basis of his own desire but also on the basis of divine guidance: "The Lord was at work in this" (Judg. 14:4). Such guidance ran counter to the time-honored commandment given to Israel concerning pagan people: "When the Lord your God brings you into the land which you are entering to occupy and drives out many nations before you . . . you must put them to death. You must not make a treaty with them or spare them. You must not intermarry with them, neither giving your daughters to their sons nor taking their daughters for your sons" (Deut. 7:1–3). It was for this reason that Samson's father, Manoa, pleaded with Samson to choose an Israelite woman rather than a Philistine (Judg. 14:3). But we are plainly told that it really was "of the Lord" that Samson should marry the woman at Timnath.

The problem that later developed was that Samson, having had such special guidance once, apparently *presumed* upon it and continued on his own to choose women from among the Gentiles: first the harlot at Gaza, and finally, Delilah. And as is commonly known, through his self-betrayal to Delilah, he found himself blinded and enslaved by the Philistines.

Samson's experience pinpoints the danger inherent in recognizing that in special circumstances the voice of God may direct us to transcend time-honored moral guidelines or laws. We may grow overconfident or arrogant, assuming that our own impulses are, without exception, sent from God. As in Samson's case, the result may be personal disaster.

Samson's story did not end, however, while he was "eyeless in Gaza at the mill with slaves."[7] The lords of the Philistines decided to celebrate their victory over Samson by holding a huge sacrifice and festival for their god Dagon. When they were in the full flush of rejoicing, they decided to crown the occasion by making the Hebrew champion of God, Samson, perform circus feats of strength. So they sent to the prison-house to bring Samson to the festival for their entertainment.

Imagine the conflict in the imprisoned Samson's mind when he received their summons! His hair had begun to grow as soon as Delilah had shaved it from him, and with the return of his hair had come a gradual return of strength. It pained Samson enough that his strength, once dedicated to God, was serving God's enemies. But now they were ordering him to do the very thing that had landed him in such deadly trouble in the first place. He was being ordered by the Philistines to break a time-honored and frequently repeated commandment to Israel: "You are not to bow down to their gods, nor worship them, nor observe their rites, but you shall tear down all their images and smash their sacred pillars" (Exod. 23:24). There could be no question that providing entertainment at a festival dedicated to Dagon constituted service to a pagan god and therefore violated this commandment. Samson had already experienced the consequences of violating general commandments on the basis of private impulse. Private impulse, he had learned, could not be trusted as an unerring guide. And if he was strong enough to perform feats of strength, he was strong enough to put up effective resistance to appearing at the festival. So Samson knew that his appearance would have to be his own responsibility. Because he had the strength to resist, he could not excuse himself by saying that he had no choice and was forced to obey orders.

Samson chose to appear at the festival. And again, although he violated one of the most fundamental Jewish commandments, his choice was genuinely "of the Lord." God strengthened him to such a degree that he was able to tear down the supporting pillars of the festival hall, killing more than three thousand of the Philistine elite. He lost his own life in the process, but he died with the satisfaction of knowing that he was once again the champion of the Lord God.

SECURE CERTAINTIES VERSUS COMPASSIONATE INVOLVEMENT

Samson's story is not a comfortable one for persons who are concerned with ethical and moral certainty. It demonstrates the tremendous risk we run of substituting our subjective impulses for the voice of God prompting us from within. But it also demonstrates the equally great risk of playing it "safe" and sticking to the tried-and-true rules of the past. Judging by Samson's story and also by Huckleberry Finn's and by the apostle Peter's, it appears that *nothing* can safely relieve us of the complexities of moral responsibility concerning any social issue, including the issue of homosexuality.

Those who urge us to self-indulgently "do our own thing" commit the error of forgetting our responsibility to community, to society, to God-within-ourselves-and-within-others-and-above-us-all. Those who urge us to preserve our private reputations by separating ourselves from human concerns make the same mistake, but for opposite reasons. In the context of Christ's story of the man fallen among thieves (Luke 10:30–37), the "do your own thing" crowd would encourage us to leave the poor man groaning in the ditch because we don't feel like helping him and because there are more pleasant ways to spend our time. The champions of private reputation would encourage us to leave the poor man groaning in the ditch in order to avoid the appearance of evil and the guilt-by-association that might accrue to us if our robes were full of dirt and blood. Either way, the result is the same: human pain is ignored and unalleviated.

The issue of homosexuality involves an enormous amount of human suffering. It is far easier to clutch our righteous robes around us and pass by on the far side of the road than to become actively involved in attempting to alleviate some of that suffering. Many church groups have in the past chosen the path of self-righteous non-involvement. So have many individuals. But Christ feels the human pain of those whose needs we have rejected, and His voice reminds us from eternity, "I tell you this: anything you did not do for one of these, however humble, you did not do for me" (Matt. 25:45).

WHAT ABOUT THE "WEAKER BRETHREN"?

Those who advocate the preservation of a stainless reputation as the top priority of the moral life frequently refer to Paul's remarks about the "weaker brethren" for support. According to 1 Cor. 8:7-13, they point out, Christians must avoid even the appearance of evil in order to keep from leading astray the undeveloped or unenlightened consciences of immature Christians. The apostle Paul does indeed make a very persuasive case in that passage reminding us that we are Christians-in-community, not simply individualists doing our own thing. Eating food consecrated to idols means nothing whatsoever to his own conscience, Paul says, because he knows that "a false god has no existence in the real world. There is no god but one." The mature Christian knows, continues Paul, that "there is one God, the Father, from whom all being comes, towards whom we move; and there is one Lord, Jesus Christ, through whom all things came to be, and we through him" (8:4-6). But the catch is that not every Christian is mature enough to be aware that idols are nothing and that God is all in all. And precisely because of our oneness in God from whom we all came and toward whom we all move, we cannot be callous toward those who are less enlightened than ourselves.

The principle is sterling. It cannot be ignored by any Christian worthy of the name. But there is a problem—and, as usual, the problem is one of implementation. Some Christians have gone so far in their interpretation of this passage that they have lived their whole lives trying never to do anything of which any other Christian might disapprove. One leader of a denomination where the "weaker brethren" looked down on theater, for instance, sat in his London hotel room rather than accept a free ticket to a performance of a Shakespearean play at the famous theater in Stratford on Avon. His reason: someone back in the United States might somehow find out that he had attended a theater, and might not be able to distinguish a play of Shakespeare's from the worst trash offered in the worst theater elsewhere. Such desperate concern for the opinions of others can bring about deafness to God's voice whenever that voice begins to direct toward new or unfamiliar practices within the Body of Christ. (The same gentleman who avoided theater for the sake of the "weaker brethren" frowned on missionary use of new technological devices like television and cassette tapes—yet he did not frown on the more familiar use of an airplane to *get* to the mission field!)

Had Peter thought only about the "weaker brethren" among the circumcised Christians, he would never have gone to a Gentile house to preach the gospel. What he actually did do suggests an alternative to Paul's conclusion in 1 Cor. 8:13. Instead of giving up whatever might be offensive to the "weaker brother," it is possible to follow Peter's example and educate the conscience of the "weaker brother" so that he or she will no longer be so easily offended. That's what Peter did when he explained his reasons to the circumcised Christians in Jerusalem.

The unbreakable principle in 1 Corinthians, chapter 8, is that mature Christians cannot live their lives in blithe unconcern for those who may be less enlightened than they. But there are two ways of handling the unenlightened conscience: either *defer* to it by avoiding what would offend it so as not to lead the other person into spiritual difficulties or *enlighten and educate* it as Peter did. Obviously, what Huck Finn needed was for someone to come along and enlighten his conscience so that he could have rejoiced in what he was doing for his friend. But of course *Huckleberry Finn* is a comic novel, not a Christian treatise, and such enlightenment was outside the scope of Mark Twain's purpose.

SOME APOSTOLIC EXAMPLES

To reassure ourselves that we are not violating the spirit of Paul's ideas in 1 Corinthians by suggesting a program of education for weaker consciences, we can look at several instances of Paul's own behavior toward those with less refined consciences than his own. As is implied in the story of Peter's vision and his subsequent preaching to the Gentiles, there was much turmoil in the early church concerning whether Gentiles who converted to Christianity should have to undergo circumcision and live according to Jewish customs. In Acts 16:3 we see Paul following his own principle of deferring to those of weaker conscience. He wanted to take Timothy with him on a missionary journey, but it was widely known that Timothy's father was Greek; so Paul "circumcised him out of consideration for the Jews who lived in those parts." But on another occasion, Paul refused to circumcise Titus, and when Peter drew back and separated himself from the Gentiles "because he was afraid of the advocates of circumcision," Paul accused him of hypocrisy and "opposed him to his face, because he was clearly in the wrong" (Galatians 2:3–14). Paul stood up in public and educated Peter's conscience (and, by extension, the consciences of those who were pressuring Peter for Jewish Christians to withdraw from uncircumcised Christians): "If you, a Jew born and bred, live like a Gentile, and not like a Jew, how can you insist that Gentiles must live like Jews?" We know from this that educating "weaker brethren" is perfectly in order.

John Calvin introduces another helpful distinction concerning Christian liberty and the "weaker brethren." He explains that we must distinguish between *offense given* and *offense taken*. If, for instance, certain Christians were to be rash or wanton in their public behavior (perhaps making thoughtless jokes about abortion or oral-genital sex or some other topic on which some Christians are very sensitive), that would be offense given. But if certain Christians were to speak carefully and responsibly on a sensitive topic, and other persons became offended because of malevolence or prejudice within themselves, that would be offense taken. Calvin says that those offended or hurt in the first case are the true "weaker brethren." Those offended in the second case are simply "ill-tempered and Pharisaical." He suggests that although we are responsible for restraining ourselves in deference to the ignorance and lack of skill of the true "weaker brethren," we are *not* responsible for pleasing "the austerity of Pharisees."[8]

From the apostle Paul's behavior and from Calvin's distinction between offense given and offense taken, it is clear that even in reference to the "weaker brother," there is no simplistic knee-jerk reaction that will relieve us from the responsibility of moral choice. Whether we like it or not, we are responsible for evaluating each situation in order to discover the most appropriate response. Through attention to the dialogue between the Bible and the best insights of human research, we stand the best chance of enlightening our own consciences so that we will have light to share with others. The quiet inner prompting of God's Spirit will take care of the rest.

3. The Homosexual as Samaritan

WHEN JESUS answered the question "Who is my neighbor?" by telling the story of a Samaritan's compassion for a wounded traveler, many listeners were disturbed that Jesus should choose a Samaritan as the model of loving behavior. Taught to despise their neighbors in Samaria, they must have found it difficult even to *imagine* such an entity as a "good" Samaritan. Samaritans were considered people with whom one should "have no dealings" (John 4:9), people who deserved to have the fire of heaven called down upon their heads (Luke 9:54).

Don't you know that, Jesus? Couldn't you have used a better example to teach neighborly love? One of *us* could have been the model! Don't you realize, Jesus, that people prefer heroes like themselves—people they can identify with? Why did you ever speak so positively about somebody from a discreditable alien group? We'd like to keep them at as great a distance from us as possible! Such thoughts as these must have passed through the minds of many that day as Jesus tried to teach them what love is all about.

And it is likely that similar thoughts passed through the minds of some persons nearly twenty centuries later with the discovery of the homosexual orientation of the Vietnam veteran whose quick thinking was credited with saving the life of President Gerald Ford in a 1975 San Francisco assassination attempt. A *homosexual* hero? Impossible. (A good *Samaritan?* Preposterous!) Somehow it didn't seem to fit the stereotypes, the familiar preconceptions about "those people"—people we keep at a distance, people who aren't "like us." It was rumored in the news media that government officials were somewhat embarrassed by the ex-Marine's gay activist associations. His heroic efforts were not rewarded with quite the same fanfare that might otherwise have been the case. (At the same time, reports indicated that the exposure of his secret sexual orientation caused him grief among his relatives.)[1]

MEMBERS OF A DIFFERENT SPECIES?

People tend to think of homosexual persons as so different and so far removed from the norm that it's almost as though they belong to a different species or come from another planet. Or, if human at all, homosexuals are considered so strange or depraved or sick or sinful that "respectable" people will be sure to keep them at a distance. Social commentator Pierre Berton has pointed his finger at Christians in this regard, charging that although churches have a tendency to "cast out the outcasts" in general, the homosexual is more outcast than anyone else. Berton writes, "A very good case can be made out that the homosexual is the modern equivalent of the leper."[2] In one midwestern city, for instance, some pastors and church members were so adamant in their fight against a city ordinance that would guarantee homosexual civil rights that they bought radio time and newspaper space and collected thousands of signatures on a petition urging Christians to "shun the sodomites and their supporters" and to purge the community of homosexual activity. "I felt like somebody hated me, and I couldn't understand it," commented one lesbian. "I felt this must be a group of people who knew nothing of homosexuals as *people*. They didn't want us to be able to get jobs or have clothing or food or housing. That must be hating."[3]

An attitude of disdain for homosexuals without consideration for them as human beings is, as we have already observed, often evident in various Christian sermons and writings. Although we are frequently reminded that we should "love the sinner while hating the sin," the disgust and disdain felt usually obliterate this distinction. For instance, one radio preacher punctuated an entire sermon with some variation on the refrains, "Sodom and Gomorrah were turned into ashes as an example of how *God* feels about being gay," and, "God dropped an atomic bomb on Sodom and Gomorrah because they were perverts!" The pastor emphasized that the ashes of these cities are the best witness concerning "how God feels about the gay community" and He reminded listeners that the Old Testament taught that homosexuals "ought to die by capital punishment." At the sermon's conclusion, the pastor's evangelistic appeal centered around the idea that Lot was a righteous man who chose God's way of escape rather than remaining in Sodom to die with such people. Listeners were admonished to think about how terrible it would be to be forced to associate with homosexuals in eternal hell. He urged his audience to accept God's gift of salvation—or else "go to hell with these people you can't stand."[4] By such sermonizing, the pastor was doing something even more serious than increasing homophobia. He was increasing the insecurity and fearfulness of every man, woman, and child who was listening by reinforcing their sense of isolation and alienation from their deepest selves, where the human family is able to recognize its oneness.

A similar view of disdain for homosexuals comes through in statements by marriage counselors Tim and Beverly LaHaye.

They argue that the Christian's attitude toward homosexuality should be based on the remembrance that "homosexuality seems to be the ultimate sin in the Bible that causes God to give men up." They also comment that "the children of Israel were commanded by God to stone to death homosexuals (Lev. 20:13), a severe treatment intended to keep them from becoming contagious."[5]

"These people you can't stand." These people who are "contagious." If we accept such views, it might seem that the world would be better off if it were rid of all homosexuals. Obviously, this was the belief of the Nazis, who sent tens of thousands of persons suspected of homosexuality to concentration camps in Germany and Austria, where, like the Jews, they were made to wear an identifying emblem, in their case a pink or lavender triangle. Large numbers of them perished.[6]

HOMOSEXUAL CONTRIBUTIONS TO CIVILIZATION

We have expressed our opinion and our hope that most Christians today would not call for such drastic measures as internment or purges. The question, Would the world be better off without homosexuals? needs to be replaced with this one: Am I able to recognize the positive good that has come to the world through homosexual persons?

Among the male "good Samaritans"—that is, male homosexuals who have made important contributions to the good of humankind—we may number Erasmus (1466–1536), the greatest scholar of his age, a brilliant author, and editor of an excellent Greek New Testament; Leonardo da Vinci (1452–1519), the great painter who gave us *The Last Supper*, with its moving portrait of Christ; Christopher Marlowe (1564–1593), Elizabethan dramatist and poet, best known for his play, *Dr. Faustus;* James I of England (1566–1625), who commissioned the translation of the Bible that bears his name; Sir Francis Bacon (1561–1626), outstanding jurist, essayist, and scientific theorist; Thomas Gray (1716–1771), author of the beloved "Elegy Written in a Country Churchyard"; Frederick the Great (1712–1786), who welcomed the persecuted Huguenots to Prussia and abolished press censorship and torture; Peter I. Tchaikovsky (1840–1893), the great composer whose *Pathétique* symphony was dedicated to the nephew he loved; Vaslav Nijinsky (1890–1950), perhaps the greatest dancer who ever lived; Marcel Proust (1871–1922), the renowned author of *Remembrance of Things Past;* A. E. Housman (1859–1936), the greatest Latin scholar of his day and an outstanding poet; T. E. Lawrence (1888–1935), best known as Lawrence of Arabia; Walt Whitman (1819–1892), one of America's greatest poets; and Henry James (1843–1916), one of America's most outstanding novelists.[7]

Among the female "good Samaritans"—lesbians who have made important contributions to humankind—are physician James Miranda Barry (c. 1795–1865), the first British woman doctor, who successfully served the British government all her working life disguised as a man; Willa Cather (1876–1947), an outstanding American novelist; Mary II (1689–1694), Queen of England, Scotland, and Ireland—the Mary of "William and Mary" (apparently William was also homosexual); Charlotte Cushman (1816–1876), memorable actress, famous for her sensitive portrayals of Hamlet, Romeo, and other male leads; Rosa Bonheur (1822–1899), the great artist who gave us *The Horse Fair* and other magnificent paintings; Margaret Fuller (1810–1850), brilliant transcendentalist author, editor, and poet; Mary Emma Woolley (d. 1947), president of Mount Holyoke College from 1900 to 1937 and one of the first American woman diplomats; Edith Hamilton (1867–1963), outstanding classical scholar, author of *The Greek Way, The Prophets of Israel,* and other books, who lived with Doris Reid for forty-seven years; and Carey Thomas (1857–1935), for many years the dean and president of Bryn Mawr College. (Profoundly spiritual and strongly influenced by her aunt, Hannah Whitall Smith, Carey Thomas lived with and loved Mary Garrett from 1904 until Mary's death in 1915.)[8]

THE NEED FOR CAUTION

We have provided the above list for the sake of those who have previously been unaware that many homosexuals live responsible, productive lives and make impressive contributions to society. But now we would like to issue a warning. Sometimes, in an effort to create sympathy for homosexuals, people attempt to enlist the names of famous persons without any definite evidence concerning their sexual orientation. For instance, novelist Virginia Woolf is frequently referred to as a lesbian; but she may simply have been asexual. We have seen no specific evidence of sexual response during her friendship with Vita Sackville-West (a known bisexual), so we prefer to make no claim concerning her.

Shakespeare has frequently been labeled homosexual because he wrote sonnets to a "fair young man" whom he addressed as "the master-mistress of my passion." In the twentieth century, such an address might constitute reasonable proof; but not so during the Renaissance, when idealized friendship was frequently expressed in passionate terminology. The fact is that Shakespeare was enthusiastically heterosexual. He casually corroborated that fact when he wrote in the very same "master-mistress" sonnet that to Shakespeare's great regret, Nature had endowed his friend with "one thing to my purpose nothing." Punning as he loved to do, Shakespeare sighed that since Nature had "prick'd thee out for women's pleasure," Shakespeare could share the man's friendship but not his body. In other words, Shakespeare wished that a creature so beautiful had been made a woman, but he was not interested in a homosexual liaison.[9]

Because of her poem "Goblin Market," which exalts the love between sisters, Christina Rossetti has been claimed by lesbians as one of their own. Certainly she was a marvelous Christian poet who deserves a much wider audience in our time. But our research indicates that although she never married—she twice broke engagements for religious reasons—she may have rejected human love simply out of an all-consuming love for Christ. On the other hand, we do find it puzzling that so many of her love poems refer to the beloved as "she" rather than "he." At least one poem, "Annie," seems impossible to interpret apart from a lesbian context. In the absence of biographical corroboration, however, and because we do not think single persons should be hounded about their sexuality, we refuse to make assumptions about Christina Rossetti.

To cite another example: some Christians have been trying to create sympathy for homosexuals by claiming that the great English poet John Milton, author of *Paradise Lost,* was homosexual. They can be forgiven for their error, since a highly respected scholarly journal had carried an article asserting that Milton's youthful relationship with Charles Diodati was a homosexual one.[10] But the evidence seems shaky, at best. Furthermore, language loses its meaning if we assert homosexual orientation in a man who remarried after his first wife's death, remarried again after the death of his second wife, and lived with his third wife until his own death, and who showed every evidence in his poetic imagery of being attracted to female rather than to male beauty. It is true that Milton did not marry until he was thirty-four; and unlike other Cambridge undergraduates, he did not frequent prostitutes. But we would not want to fall into the stylish trap of assuming that either celibacy or close friendship automatically spells homosexuality.

In our list of homosexual men and women who have made outstanding contributions to society, we have included only those for whom strong evidence points toward lifelong homosexual orientation and/or activity. Our list is of course very sketchy and far from complete. Since most homosexuals married because of social pressure, many persons on our list were married; but letters, diaries, or other contemporary evidence indicates that the marriages were more or less in name only. We have omitted persons who apparently *enjoyed* sexual relations with both sexes, such as Madame de Staël and Lord Byron, because they were bisexuals, not homosexuals.

HOMOSEXUAL CHRISTIANS

Some of the persons in our list were obviously homosexual *Christians*, not just in a nominal sense, but in a very heartfelt one. The term *homosexual Christian* is a jarring one to those who claim that it is impossible to be both Christian and homosexual. It can easily strike certain people in the way that the thought of a "good Samaritan" struck Christ's first-century audience. However, as Margaret Evening has written:

> It is often the case that the homosexual is a very loving and lovable person with a tremendous contribution to make. . . . If people wish to regard homosexuality as a freak of nature, and even if it is not the condition ordained by God when He said that it was not good for man to dwell alone, then we can only rejoice that God is, as ever, bringing good out of evil. We can thus accept with humility the special gifts mediated to us through those who are His homosexual children, our brothers and sisters whom we cannot and would not disown.[11]

Since some Christians may want to counter Margaret Evening's statement by asserting that God *has* no homosexual children, it may help to look more closely at several concrete examples.

First, let us take an imaginary journey to Rome and stand before Michelangelo's sculpture, *The Pieta,* to gaze in awe upon the Savior who died for our sins, his crucified body lying across the lap of his mourning mother. Touched by the beauty of the scene and the sensitivity of the artist, we are moved to worship God. Later, we marvel at Michelangelo's skill in bringing the biblical drama to life through the frescoes on the ceiling of the Sistine Chapel. At still another time, we are impressed by some of his sonnets of devotion to the Lord.

Then, in the midst of our journey, we find out that Michelangelo was homosexual. What are we going to do with this information? Deny the authenticity of his Christianity? Deny the value of his contributions? Would we want to say that the world and the church would be better off had it been rid of *him?*

Such questions may continue to haunt us as we move on to other examples. We are impressed and challenged with the depth and insight of W. H. Auden's Christmas oratorio, *For the Time Being,* and we wonder how—if all the negative stereotypes are true—a self-confessed homosexual could have put into the mouth of Simeon such words as these concerning the Incarnation:

But here and now the word which is implicit in the Beginning and in the End is immediately explicit, and that which hitherto we could only passively fear as the incomprehensible I AM, henceforth we may actively love with comprehension that THOU ART. Wherefore, having seen Him, not in some prophetic vision of what might be, but with the eyes of our own weakness as to what actually is, we are bold to say that we have seen our salvation. . . . And because of His visitation, we may no longer desire God as if He were lacking: our redemption is no longer a question of pursuit but of surrender to Him who is always and everywhere present. Therefore at every moment we pray that, following Him, we may depart from our anxiety into His peace.[12]

Or we might think of the nineteenth-century priest, Gerard Manley Hopkins. In a 1977 *Christianity Today* article, Matthew Brown rightly assessed Hopkins as "a writer of 'exploding poetry' par excellence," who "did it to the glory of God." Brown called special attention to Hopkins's "The Wreck of the *Deutschland,*" correctly describing it as a poem "universally Christian," because "Christ is at its center and holds this chaotic world together, providing hope."[13] Yet shortly before this conservative Christian periodical printed Brown's article extolling the Christian life and message of Gerard Manley Hopkins, *The Hopkins Quarterly* had published an article on the homosexual orientation of Hopkins and its influence on his works.[14] Hopkins, a Jesuit, lived celibate; but his poetic images make clear that the beauty that tempted him was *male* beauty.

We would enjoy providing multitudes of examples of the poetic gift and the total Christian devotion of Gerard Manley Hopkins. But space limits us to just one example, and we have chosen the delightful poem entitled "Pied Beauty":

> Glory be to God for dappled things—
> For skies of couple-colour as a brinded cow;
> For rose-moles all in stipple upon trout that swim;
> Fresh-firecoal chestnut-falls; finches' wings;
> Landscape plotted and pieced—fold, fallow, and plough;
> And áll trádes, their gear and tackle and trim.
> All things counter, original, spare, strange;
> Whatever is fickle, freckled (who knows how?)
> With swift, slow; sweet, sour; adazzle, dim;
> He fathers-forth whose beauty is past change:
> Praise him.[15]

It should be obvious that Christianity would be impoverished by the loss of the contributions of Hopkins and Auden and Michelangelo.

CONTEMPORARY HOMOSEXUALS IN THE CHURCH

Among our contemporaries, a few homosexual Christians have made their orientation public, while still trying to maintain their ties to the church and the Christian community as a whole. Episcopal priest Ellen Marie Barrett explains that her relationship with her lesbian partner, a long-term and faithful one, is "what feeds the strength and compassion I bring to the ministry." Ms. Barrett commented privately to one of us that Christians seem willing enough to ordain into the ministry homosexuals who feel guilty, furtive, and ashamed about their homosexuality, but seem outraged at the prospect of ordaining those who fully accept their sexual orientation and live faithfully with their chosen partner. This has the effect, she said, of proclaiming that *neurotic* homosexuals make acceptable priests while *healthy* homosexuals do not.

At Ms. Barrett's ordination ceremony, a priest named James Wattley said that Ms. Barrett's lesbianism rendered her ordination a "travesty and a scandal." But Bishop Paul Moore testified that Ms. Barrett was "highly qualified intellectually, morally, and spiritually to be a priest." Bishop Moore also noted that "many persons of homosexual tendencies are presently in the ordained ministry."[16]

Indeed, the Archbishop of Canterbury startled the world several years ago with his public acknowledgment that a large number of homosexuals are to be found within the ranks of the Anglican clergy.[17] And in June, 1972, a letter in the *Baptist Times* asking for letters from Baptist ministers who are homosexual elicited a considerable response and revealed a profound need for contact with others of like mind.[18] Elizabeth Moberly, an Oxford University research fellow, asserts that "not only are homosexuals numerous generally, but it would seem that a particularly high percentage of them are to be found within the church."[19]

One such person is James D. Anderson, an elder in the Broadway Presbyterian Church of New York City, who has served on the Board of National Missions in Alaska and as secretary of Presbytery's Committee on Mission. Says Anderson, who has lived in a committed homosexual relationship for over five years: "If the church is to fully do its job of reconciliation among people and between the human family and God, it must support gay people by helping them accept their sexuality and to express it lovingly. Needless to say, the church cannot do this without full acceptance of gay people themselves as healthy and complete persons."[20]

Another such person must remain anonymous because she is studying in a fundamentalist environment from which she would be ostracized if her homosexuality became public knowledge. She formerly studied with Dr. Francis Schaeffer in L'Abri, Switzerland, and hopes to enter active Christian service at the completion of her studies. In an unpublished autobiographical sketch, she describes the past several years of her life. The lesbian feminist community which she mentions is an extremely radical segment of the larger women's movement.

> I went back and forth between the Christian community and the lesbian feminist community. I was never totally satisfied with either. The Christian community offered truth and some sense of direction. The lesbian feminist community offered support, love, and a deep caring for one another. . . . There is a deeper sense of community in the [secular] women's movement than there is in the church. . . . The Christian community seems to be more concerned with a respectable appearance than acting with compassion and responsibility. The church is not reaching out in love, it is erecting steel barricades.

Reading this, it is hard not to remember the priest and the Levite who kept their robes clean and their images respectable by walking on the far side of the road to avoid the man who had fallen among thieves!

Another homosexual Christian, Joyce Liechenstein, has worked in the Presbyterian church for twenty-six years, nine of those in the post of Director of Christian Education. She comments: "I came to understand that God is a loving God; it makes no sense that God would reject me simply for being homosexual. The scriptures make it clear in Genesis that God's creation has unlimited variety, and we are part of that variety. God looked at his creation and saw that it was good."[21]

Father John McNeill, a Jesuit priest, has publicly affirmed his homosexual orientation although, true to his vow of chastity, he lives celibate. His book, *The Church and the Homosexual,* is a model of restraint, scholarship, and Christlike spirit. It is vital reading for anybody who wants to understand homosexuals from their own point of view and in a spiritual context.

Bill Silver, who has been planning and preparing for the Presbyterian ministry for the past fifteen years, explains that "accepting homosexuality as a good part of my life, I feel called to a ministry of proclaiming the good news of Christ to all people regardless of their sexual orientation."[22]

Rick Huskey, an ordained United Methodist deacon, had been hoping to enter the ministry of his church. But after he revealed his homosexual orientation, his church decided not to make him an elder, and later removed him from deacon's orders. Both Rick and his parents felt hurt by these decisions, but they were sustained by the supportive understanding shown by individual members of the church.[23]

Perhaps we can allow Malcolm Boyd, an Episcopal priest who, in August, 1976, made public his homosexuality, to speak on behalf of all the homosexual Christians who must keep their sexual identity secret:

They stand inside your church, Lord, and know a wholeness that can benefit it. Long ago they learned that they must regard the lilies of the field, putting their trust in you.

Pressured to hide their identities and gifts, they have served you with an unyielding, fierce love inside the same church that condemned them.

Taught that they must feel self-loathing, nevertheless they learned integrity and dignity, and how to look into your face and laugh with grateful joy, Lord.

Victims of a long and continuing torture, they asserted a stubborn faith in the justice of your kingdom.

Negativism was drummed into them as thoroughly as if they were sheet metal. They learned what it is to be hated. Yet, despite real rejection, they insisted on attesting to the fullness and beauty of all human creation, including theirs, in your image.

They are alive and well and standing inside your church. Bless them, Lord, to your service.[24]

Like it or not, we Christians can no longer avoid dealing, individually and collectively, with the issue of homosexuality. No doubt many of us may feel it distressing and unsettling to be told about the many positive contributions made by homosexuals to the ongoing life of civilization and the church. We are not used to thinking of homosexuals in such a positive light. No doubt some of us feel just the way Christ's first-century audience felt when the Lord gave them a model of lovingkindness in the shape of a despised Samaritan!

✼ 4. Stigma and Stereotyping

W E HAVE supplied some personal statements from homosexual Christians because considering homosexuality in the abstract is quite different from confronting it personally. Sometimes, unexpectedly, the issue may come even closer to home, as it did in the following cases:

1. A minister's daughter came home to announce that she had been involved in a lesbian relationship that had just broken up, leaving her crushed. Her parents were shocked. The father was unable to face either her or the issue. The mother has been trying to be supportive.

2. A promising student at a church-related college sought psychological and religious counseling concerning his homosexuality. College officials told him they had no choice except to expel him.

3. A man and a woman met at a conservative Christian college. Drawn together by their mutual devotion to Christ and by their active participation together in Christian service, they looked forward to a life of continued ministry as husband and wife. She was impressed by the respect he showed her—he didn't treat her like a sex object by pressing for physical involvement, as so many other men had seemed to do. After a few years of

marriage and one child, his confession felt like a knife passing through her entire being. He had been sexually involved with a number of men, beginning before their marriage, he said, and now felt so convinced of his homosexuality that he could no longer function as a husband. He said he loved his wife and child but needed to be released from the marriage.

4. He was an elder in a large, influential church and known for his spiritual leadership. One day, after listening to a sermon in which brief mention was made of homosexuality as a sin, he could stand it no longer. He stood up and announced that he had been living in a committed homosexual union for four years; indeed, on that very day he and his partner were celebrating their fourth anniversary. He said he yearned for the day when the church could share their joy and welcome them as a couple. The congregation was stunned. Did this call for church discipline? Should he be relieved of his office? Or should he be given the loving Christian acceptance he had requested?

5. It is Sunday morning in another city. Two men singing in the choir are partners in a "gay marriage." The pastor is convinced they should retain the privilege of serving Christ through music, but he does not feel free to grant their request for a public marriage ceremony. Some persons in the congregation accept these men as a couple; others object. Some minister friends of the pastor tell him he is wrong to be so accepting of the relationship and should be preaching on its sinfulness.

6. The call came late at night. It was Greg, Marc's roommate from seminary days, now living in a distant state. "I've got to talk with you and Kathy," he said. "I can't go on any longer without telling somebody." Suddenly he blurted out, "Marc, you're my friend; I can trust you. Even so, I'm not sure how you'll take this. I—well, I might just as well say it. *I'm a homosexual.* No, wait. Don't say anything. Just let me finish. I've suspected it for a long

time. Remember all my unloading on you about the problems I kept having with women? Well, now I know why. Yes, I *am* sure about it, and it probably sounds crazy but I feel sort of at peace about it—just admitting it to myself and you. Yet there are many problems, too—like whether to continue thinking about the ministry. Maybe it's out of the question now."

These are just a few contemporary examples from real life. Only the names and a few minor details have been changed; in fact, some of the stories are composites of several separate but amazingly similar experiences. That is why we cannot continue to dodge the issue as concerned Christians. We need to think it through.

WHY CHRISTIANS FIND THIS TOPIC SO DIFFICULT

We Christians tend to avoid thinking and talking about homosexuality in any depth for at least three reasons. There are, first, *social and psychological reasons*, including societal attitudes, anxieties about our own feelings or about what others might think of us, and more general fears about the entire topic. There are also *religious considerations*, including the matter of what the Bible does and doesn't say on the topic, questions of theology, and church traditions. Finally, there are *informational reasons*, by which we mean either inadequate knowledge or misinformation. In this and the following two chapters, let's consider these reasons for avoidance one at a time.

SOCIAL AND PSYCHOLOGICAL STIGMATIZATION

In one of the less publicized sections of Jimmy Carter's controversial 1976 *Playboy* interview, the presidential candidate told the interviewers that "the issue of homosexuality always makes me nervous." He suggested that at least two factors might contribute to his sense of uneasiness: his lack of personal knowledge on the subject, and his Baptist faith. The interviewers wondered if his uneasiness was related to the political sensitivity of the issue. "No," replied Carter, "it's more complicated than that. It's political, it's moral, and it's strange territory for me."[1]

The area of homosexuality is "strange territory" to many Christians, and the reasons are indeed complicated. Sociologist Paul Rock points out that "our ability to test information about objects in the social world diminishes as these objects become distant from us." Although we might take issue with something that was told to us about our intimate acquaintances, "we have little opportunity to dispute contentions about those who are socially distant."[2] Furthermore, as other sociologists note, the more we keep persons socially removed from us, the easier it is to think of them not as individuals but as "anonymous abstractions."[3] We can then think in terms of general characteristics which we apply to whole categories of people. The uniqueness of the individual is swallowed up in the impersonal and distorted stereotype.

The human tendency to create "anonymous abstractions" explains why homosexual persons have often lodged justified complaints about the failure of many Christian leaders to recognize the shared humanity of all persons regardless of sexual orientation. In the words of one gay activist: "There's such a tendency among Christians to lump all homosexuals together as a group of faceless, nameless 'perverts' and to make statements not rooted in fact. They don't see us as *people.*"[4] This is what Paul Rock has in mind when he says that "social distance dehumanizes our typing of people."[5] Two other sociologists describe this phenomenon in terms of a general social rule: "The greater the social distance between the typer and the person singled out for typing, the broader the type and the quicker it may be applied."[6]

Because the social distance between most persons and the homosexual community is signally wide, it becomes easy to make sweeping generalizations: "Male homosexuals are effeminate." "All lesbians are tough and masculine, and they hate men." "There's no such thing as a happy homosexual." "It's dangerous to let homosexuals work with children." "Lesbian mothers should not be permitted to have custody of their children." "Homosexuals are irresponsible workers." "Homosexuals are neurotic and immature." "All that homosexuals ever think about is sex, sex, sex!" "Homosexuals are unable to sustain a relationship; they are by nature promiscuous." "Homosexuals know nothing about love, only lust." "Homosexuals are out to convert everybody to their way of living. Give them their so-called rights and they'll destroy the family and bring about the downfall of our nation."

It must be readily admitted that sometimes gay activist leaders seem to be their own worst enemies. Males defiantly marching up the street in dresses do nothing to quiet the fears of the heterosexual world. Wearing T-shirts that advertise obscenities, or shouting rude remarks at hearings concerning gay civil rights ordinances, likewise serve to reinforce stereotypes and widen the gap between homosexuals and heterosexuals. Such behavior stems from frustration and desperation in the face of social rejection, just as frustrated ghetto dwellers will often deface property in their own neighborhoods as an expression of their feelings of powerlessness. It is also true that, in some cases, professional anti-homosexual agitators infiltrate the protest rallies in order to make the gay community appear less responsible and mature than it actually is. What the heterosexual world needs to realize is that apart from the flambouyant activists, there are literally hundreds of thousands of homosexuals who are living quiet, responsible, constructive lives.

Given the social stigma attached to homosexuality, the dehumanized typifications of homosexual persons, the social distance maintained, and the widespread social support for certain generalizations ("Everybody knows that's what they're like"), it is not surprising that most of us tend simply to accept the generalizations without question. For some reason, it doesn't occur to us that the stereotypes and the assumptions to which they give rise might be highly inaccurate. Nor does it occur to us that by repeating them we might be bearing false witness against our neighbor and that therefore we owe it to ourselves to give some serious study to the subject. After all, we worry, what might it suggest about ourselves if we showed too much interest in obtaining more information? And what might others think? Curiosity and a desire to learn all we can about a subject are usually considered commendable, but somehow we don't feel that way about this particular subject. It's set apart and we fear it. Furthermore, there are the librarians and bookstore clerks to think about. We feel timid and awkward about asking them for "those" books!

SOME HELPFUL BOOKS

However, books are one of the most helpful ways of bridging the social distance—not only books that provide information from a scientific standpoint, but also books that can help us understand the human element. In this latter category are two novels that have been published in recent years. *Patience and Sarah* is the story of two nineteenth-century women who loved each other and spent a lifetime together in a homosexual union, based on a true incident.[7] And *Consenting Adult* is the story of a young man's confession of his homosexuality and the struggle of his parents for many years as they try to come to terms with it.[8] A nonfiction book specifically intended to acquaint heterosexual readers with the joys, fears, struggles, achievements, and everyday life of homosexual persons as "real people" is *Familiar*

Faces, Hidden Lives by the late Howard Brown, M.D. During Mayor John Lindsay's administration, Dr. Brown had served as New York City's first health services administrator. After a heart attack in 1972, at the age of 48, this highly respected physician decided that, in what little time he had left, he would work "to free future generations of homosexuals from the agony of secrecy and the constant need to hide."[9] He announced publicly that he was a homosexual and began work on the book that was published after his death.

From another viewpoint comes a book published by a conservative Christian press. Entitled *The Returns of Love* (a title adapted from the work of the homosexual American poet, Walt Whitman),[10] it consists of a series of letters describing the inner turmoil of a young man endeavoring to overcome his homosexual impulses and live a celibate life, which he feels is the only way to please Christ. His agony is evident as he speaks of his loneliness and bares his heart in candor:

> Peter, can you understand it? This is the impossibility of the situation—what I may have I don't want, and what I do want I may not have. I want a friend, but more than a friend; I want a wife. But I don't want a woman.[11]

Reading books such as these may be disturbing, and there may be much in them with which we disagree or find troublesome as Christians. But if we really want to understand and reach out in *agapé* love to the homosexual, these books can be a great step toward a personal acquaintance with the human aspect of the question.

WHAT IF A FRIEND OR RELATIVE IS GAY?

Those who wish to maintain the social gap between themselves and homosexuals (even from the indirect acquaintanceship provided by books) find it especially difficult when confronted with homosexuality in a friend or relative. After all, we have been taught to regard homosexuality as "deviancy," a violation of acceptable standards. Again to quote Rock: "Instead of feeling that the moral and social gulf that separates us from deviancy is diminished when we make such a discovery, we frequently impose this gulf between ourselves and our redefined acquaintance." We then reconstruct our image of the individual. A stereotype may come to mind so that we think we now know everything about that person and can see what he or she "really was all along." And we tend to forget everything about the person that commanded our love and respect before the revelation.[12]

The result is often ostracism. "We daily affirm our moralities and value structures by placing ourselves apart from others whom we regard as deviant," writes sociologist N. K. Denzin.[13] Such rejection then drives the homosexual person even farther from us, and the cycle continues, as the social distance again facilitates thinking of the person in abstract, depersonalized terms ("he/she is a homosexual, you know; no need to bother with further information"). Psychiatrist Armand Nicholi II of Harvard Medical School calls attention to the harm that can come when the church displays such an attitude: "The homosexual often encounters an insensitive ear and a closed door within the Christian community. Such a reaction intensifies the anguish, the pervasive loneliness, and utter despondency that haunt him and not infrequently leads to his suicide."[14]

Disclosure of an acquaintance's homosexuality doesn't always lead to rejection. Instead of pushing the person as far from us as the subject has always been before, we may find ourselves bringing the subject as close to us as the person has been. When that happens, we examine the topic with new eyes. That's what happened to the mother in the novel *Consenting Adult.* Her love for her son led her, over a period of many years, to study and rethink homosexuality until finally she could accept him as he was. Passing through some kind of "heart-changing personal experience," says sociologist Erving Goffman, is a common occurance "before taking the standpoint of those with a particular stigma."[15]

COGNITIVE DISSONANCE

Still, it is not likely to be easy. As we mentioned in Chapter 2, the apostle Peter found it extremely difficult to accept the vision sent to teach him that God was ready to welcome the Gentiles. "No, Lord, no," he cried, feeling inner turmoil at the very idea of going against the principles of right and wrong as he had heard them all his life. The psychological concept of "cognitive dissonance" is useful here.[16] In music, when two notes don't "fit together" to produce harmony, the resulting sound is called dissonance. Similarly, a clash occurs in our minds and emotions when two pieces of knowledge are hard to reconcile. For instance: (1) We learn that our acquaintance, whom we consider a very "good" person, is homosexual. (2) We have been taught to think of homosexual persons as "bad." These two facts clash, causing inner dissonance, which we may seek to resolve in some way or another. Perhaps we'll begin changing our attitudes toward our friend (for example, cooling off the friendship). Perhaps we'll begin changing our ideas about homosexuality (like the mother in the novel). Perhaps we'll try to change our friend (for example, recommending psychiatric treatment or prayer for deliverance from homosexual desires). Or perhaps we'll try to quiet the inner tension by ignoring or denying what we know.

This last course was the one chosen by one of Michelangelo's contemporary admirers, Ascanio Condivi. Because he equated homosexuality with lewdness and shameful lust and could think of it in no other terms, Condivi found it impossible to believe that

Michelangelo could be homosexual. He argued that only "the most honest of words" issued from Michelangelo's mouth and "no evil thoughts were born in him." How could a man be pure minded and profoundly Christian and yet be erotically drawn toward the same sex? But Condivi could not deny Michangelo's deeply Christian spirit, with which he had had personal contact. Therefore, it was the homosexuality that had to be denied; and this Condivi tried desperately to do.[17]

Sometimes the cognitive dissonance is felt in the homosexual person's own being. Dr. Howard Brown tells of the discovery of his own homosexual predilection at age eighteen:

> I had never met a homosexual man, or at least been aware that I had met one. But I knew what every other Midwesterner knew in 1942: Homos were mysterious, evil people, to be avoided at all costs. And I was one. Often, when I thought of this, I would break out in a cold sweat. I couldn't be. I shoved the idea aside.[18]

Persons endeavoring to live as homosexual Christians find the problem particularly acute. Novelist Christopher Isherwood lived for years in a homosexual relationship with W. H. Auden. During the Modern Language Association meetings in New York in 1974, Isherwood told an audience that Auden suffered greatly all his life from the fact that he could not work out what he felt to be a satisfactory harmony between his Christianity and his homosexuality. Perhaps this is one reason Auden thought and wrote so much about guilt and the nature of sin.[19] Yet by the grace of God and despite the personal pain caused by the attitudes of many Christians, Auden was able to leave us such excellent poetry as this:

> We belong to our kind,
> Are judged as we judge . . .
> Finite in fact yet refusing to be real,

Wanting our own way, unwilling to say Yes
To the Self-So which is the same at all times,
That Always-Opposite which is the whole subject
Of our not-knowing, yet from no necessity
Condescended to exist and to suffer death
And, scorned on a scaffold, ensconced in His life
The human household. In our anguish we struggle
To elude Him, to lie to Him, yet His love observes
His appalling promise; His predilection
As we wander and weep is with us to the end.[20]

Auden's struggles bring us to what is without a doubt the single most important factor in the difficulties most Christians have with the topic of homosexuality: the Bible as it has been interpreted for centuries.

❦ 5. What Does the Bible Say?

THE BIBLE does not have a great deal to say about homosexuality, and in the original languages the term itself is never used. Whenever homosexual acts are mentioned, the acts are always committed in a very negative context, such as adultery, promiscuity, violence, or idolatrous worship. The fact that this negative context is often ignored may explain why Christians have traditionally shown harsh, unloving, often cruel attitudes toward homosexual persons.

The destruction of Sodom and Gomorrah, described in Genesis, chapter 19, is a case in point. As we noted earlier, this story has often been interpreted as showing God's abhorrence of homosexuality. Two angels in the form of men were sent to Sodom and were invited into the home of Lot, described in the New Testament as "a good man, shocked by the dissolute habits of the lawless society in which he lived" (2 Pet. 2:7–8). Lot showed the angels warm hospitality, as was the custom, but was stunned by the rude and violent behavior exhibited by his neighbors toward the guests. All the men of the city, "both young and old, surrounded the house—everyone without exception" and demanded to see his visitors. "Bring them out," they shouted, "so that we can have intercourse with them" (Gen. 19:5). When Lot begged the men to leave his guests alone and take his two virgin daughters instead, the men angrily refused and stormed the door, only to be struck blind by the angels.

Lot and his family were warned to flee. In order for the city to be spared, according to Gen. 18:32, ten righteous men had to be found. By this sordid incident God's prior decision to destroy the city was shown to be fully justified.

It should be noted that some Bible scholars do not believe that the intent of the men of Sodom was sexual. They have pointed out that the Hebrew word translated "know" (or "intercourse" as in the New English Bible quoted above) can mean simply communication—in this case, a desire to examine the strangers' credentials.[1] Whether the intent was sexual or not, however, the strangers were treated abominably and the sin of inhospitality was committed—one more instance of the city's wickedness that called forth God's righteous judgment.

There is no denying that the incident has long been associated in the minds of most people with homosexuality. Indeed, the word *sodomy* is derived from this biblical passage. (Sodomy statutes are notorious in their ambiguity. Technically, sodomy refers to anal intercourse, and in England the word is understood exclusively in that sense.[2] In the United States, legislative use of the term varies. In some states it may include sexual contact with animals and mouth-genital contact, even if such contact occurs privately between persons of the opposite sex, and even if the persons are married to each other.)[3] But if we seriously consider what the Scriptures do and do not say on the topic of homosexuality, what observations about the judgment on Sodom and Gomorrah can we responsibly make?

SODOMIZING AS HUMILIATION-BY-VIOLENCE

First, we must take note that the men of Sodom could not possibly have been exclusively homosexual in orientation in the sense that the term is used today. Quite likely, they were primarily heterosexual, out for novelty, and seeking to humiliate the strangers. For the city to have any continuing population at all, the group must have included a substantial number of husbands and fathers, since every last one of the city's males is said to have taken part in this attempted gang rape! Sodom certainly was not a "gay community" in the sense described by the radio preacher mentioned earlier in this book.

Rape is not a sexual act so much as it is an act of violence. In heterosexual rape, a man is showing his utter disdain for women. The emphasis is on displaying force and demonstrating power over someone who is perceived as weak and vulnerable.[4] Thus, among some ancient peoples, it was not unusual to flaunt one's triumph over enemies by treating them with the greatest possible contempt. Such contempt was demonstrated by forcing captive men to "take the part of a woman" and be passive recipients in anal intercourse.

A similar pattern shows up in modern prisons. "We're going to take your manhood" or "We're gonna make a girl out of you" are common assertions in such sexual assaults. Evidence of this kind of language shows up repeatedly in a 1968 study of the Philadelphia prison system. Researcher Alan J. Davis reports that "conquest and degradation" were the sexual aggressor's primary goals, along with that of retaining membership in a sexually militant group (for protection in a conquer-or-be-conquered situation, as well as for providing a sense of prestige and power). Gang rape is related to an emphasis on dominance through the subjugation of others. Davis is careful to emphasize that such incidents are totally different from incidents of *consensual* homosexuality— same-sex contact for the sake of sexual release or for the expression of love. Men who assaulted fellow prisoners did not consider themselves homosexual, nor did they even believe they had participated in homosexual acts. This denial appears to be based on what Davis calls their "startlingly primitive view of sexual relationships, one that defines as male whichever partner is aggressive and as homosexual whichever partner is passive."[5]

If the modern prison's version of a gang rape was in the minds of the men of Sodom, it is understandable that they did not accept Lot's offer of his daughters. Women already had a low place in the society of Sodom (Lot's offer is indicative of that fact). Humiliating actual women would not have provided the sense of conquest they had anticipated in degrading the male strangers and "dragging them down" to the level of women. In one parallel biblical case, however, a group of men *did* accept a female substitute, who was thrown out to them like a piece of meat to a pack of wolves (Judges, chapter 19). They sexually abused her all night long, and she died as a result, whereupon her husband cut her up into twelve pieces and sent her parts to all the tribes of Israel. This story of rape and murder is hardly rendered any more palatable by the fact that the host offered his daughter to spare his guest, and the guest presented his own wife to spare himself. In the ancient Middle East, writes Roman Catholic scholar John McKenzie, "that the woman should be sacrificed to save the man was simply taken for granted."[6] No wonder that a man would dread the disgrace and punishment of being treated "like a woman," which is what male gang rape signified.

All of this is by way of saying that rather than concentrating on homosexuality, the Sodom story seems to be focusing on two specific evils: (1) violent gang rape and (2) inhospitality to the stranger. Surely, none of us would be prepared to say that if the men of Sodom had accepted the offer of Lot's daughters and abused them as the men did in Judges, chapter 19, then God would have withheld judgment since *heterosexual* acts had taken place! Violence—forcing sexual activity upon another—is the real point of this story. To put it another way: even if the angels had taken on the form of women for their earthly visitation, the desire of the men of Sodom to rape them would have been every bit as evil in the sight of God. And the rain of fire and brimstone would have been every bit as sure.

HOW THE BIBLE INTERPRETS THE SIN OF SODOM

Concerning the inhospitality described in the Sodom story, John McNeill reminds Christians of the irony that no group has been treated *less* hospitably by the church than the homosexual community, and that the biblical passage used to justify such treatment has been the very one that condemns uncharitable attitudes toward the stranger. "In the name of a mistaken understanding of the crime of Sodom and Gomorrah, the true crime of Sodom and Gomorrah has been and continues to be repeated every day," argues McNeill.[7] To underscore the sin of inhospitality in Sodom, he reminds us of Jesus' words to his disciples in Luke 10:10–13: "When you enter a town and they do not make you welcome. . . . I tell you, it will be more bearable for Sodom on the great Day than for that town."

This brings us to a second factor to keep in mind while examining the story of Sodom: the Bible is its own best commentary on many issues. And the Bible provides explanations for Sodom's destruction that have nothing at all to do with homosexuality. In the first chapter of Isaiah, the nation of Judah is rebuked through a comparison with Sodom and Gomorrah. The specific sins mentioned are greed, rebellion against God, empty religious ritual without true devotion to God, failure to plead the cause of orphans and widows, failure to pursue justice, and failure to champion the oppressed. There is no mention of homosexuality.

In Ezek. 16:49–50 we read: "This was the iniquity of your sister Sodom: she and her daughters had pride of wealth and food in plenty, comfort and ease, and yet she never helped the poor and wretched. They grew haughty and did deeds abominable in my sight, and I made away with them, as you have seen." Although the "deeds abominable" have been assumed to include homosexual acts, here again there is no specific mention of homosexuality. The specific charge is lack of concern for the poor.

In the New Testament, as we have seen, Jesus refers to Sodom, not in the context of sexual acts, but in the context of inhospitality (Luke 10:10). Jude 7 does refer to the sexual sins of Sodom: "They committed fornication and followed unnatural lusts." The emphasis here is on heterosexual intercourse outside of marriage (fornication) and on "going after alien or other or strange flesh," as the original Greek reads in literal translation. These "unnatural lusts" thus could, in this context, and in view of the apocryphal texts to which Jude made allusion,[8] refer to a desire for sexual contact between human and heavenly beings. The Jerusalem Bible footnote for Jude 7 reads, "They lusted not after human beings, but after the strangers who were angels, Genesis 19:1–11."

If, then, we decide to follow the time-honored principles of allowing the Bible to provide its own commentary and of interpreting cloudy passages in the light of clearer ones, we are forced to admit that the Sodom story says nothing at all about the homosexual condition. The only real application to homosexuals would have to be a general one: homosexuals, like everybody else, should show hospitality to strangers, should deal justly with the poor and vulnerable, and should not force their sexual attentions upon those unwilling to receive them.

ISRAEL'S HOLINESS CODE: THE LEVITICUS PASSAGES

Most scholars agree that in the fertility religions of Israel's neighbors, male cult prostitutes were employed for homosexual acts. The people who loved and served the God of Israel were strictly forbidden to have anything to do with such idolatry, and Jewish men were commanded never to serve as temple prostitutes (Deut. 23:17–19; 1 Kings 14:24; 2 Kings 23:7).

Two Old Testament passages make explicit reference to homosexual acts. Lev. 18:23 commands, "You shall not lie with a man as with a woman: that is an abomination." And Lev. 20:13 warns: "If a man has intercourse with a man as with a woman, they both commit an abomination. They shall be put to death; their blood shall be on their own heads." These verses are part of Israel's Holiness Code, which includes commandments not to eat meat with blood in it, not to wear garments made of two kinds of yarn, not to plant fields with two kinds of seed, and not to be tattooed, as well as specific instructions on sexual matters. Forbidden activities include bestiality (sexual contact with animals), incest (sexual contact with relatives—children, parents, siblings, in-laws, and so on), male homosexual acts, adultery, and sexual intercourse with a woman during her menstrual period. The reasons given for these proscriptions involve several factors: (1) separation from other nations and their customs (Lev. 18:1–5), (2) avoidance of idolatry and any practices associated with it (Lev. 20:1–7), and (3) ceremonial uncleanness. The first two reasons are clearly related to the proscription of homosexual acts, since such practices were part of the fertility religions. But the third reason may also be relevant. Avoidance of ceremonial uncleanness clearly lay behind the requirement that intercourse be avoided during menstruation; and similarly, an emission of semen rendered men ceremonially unclean (see Lev. 15). Thus, a kind of "double uncleanness" might have been associated with male homosexual acts.

Be that as it may, consistency and fairness would seem to dictate that if the Israelite Holiness Code is to be invoked against twentieth-century homosexuals, it should likewise be invoked against such common practices as eating rare steak, wearing mixed fabrics, and having marital intercourse during the menstrual period. (See our discussion on pp. 112-115.)

It should be noticed that female homosexuality is not mentioned in the Holiness Code, even though women were certainly not ignored in the other sexual behaviors mentioned therein. Punishment is meted out to women and men alike for participating in adultery, incest, bestiality, and intercourse during menstruation. However, according to the Talmud, the only concern over sexual acts between women centered around whether or not such acts constituted a loss of virginity. If so, the women would be disqualified from possible marriage to a priest. "Women that practice lewdness with one another are unfit for the priesthood," instructed one rabbi. Evidently, there was some disagreement over this point among the rabbis, with one argument being that while a sexual relationship with a man would clearly mean loss of virginity and thus rule out marriage to a priest, "when it is that of a woman, the action is regarded as mere obscenity." Among the Jews, then, it appears that women who engaged in homosexual acts were not set apart as distinct from a number of other categories from whom priests (especially the high priest) were not permitted to choose a wife: widows, divorcees, nonvirginal women, proselytes, and emancipated slaves (Lev. 21:7, 13–14).[9]

THE UNIVERSALITY OF ROMANS 1

Lesbianism is mentioned only once in the Bible—which brings us to a discussion of the first chapter of Romans. In that chapter the apostle Paul, writing to both Jews and Gentiles, shows how sin has alienated all people from God. The Gentile world had turned from God to idols; the Jews had turned to smug self-righteousness, hypocrisy, and harsh judgments on others, in spite of their boasting in the law (Rom. 2:23). In other words, *all* of us have sinned and fallen short of the glory of God (Rom. 3:23). The point, then, of Romans, chapters 1 and 2, is not to set apart some category of persons as the worst kind of sinners possible.

The clear relationship between condemnation of homosexual practices and idolatry in the Old Testament is also evident in Romans. After giving a detailed description of a world that "exchanged the truth of God for a lie, and worshiped and served created things rather than the Creator," Paul continues:

> Because of this, God gave them over to shameful lusts. Even their women exchanged natural relations for unnatural ones. In the same way the men also abandoned natural relations with women and were inflamed with lust for one another. Men committed indecent acts with other men, and received in themselves the due penalty for their perversion. (Rom. 1:26–27, NIV).

The key thoughts seem to be lust, "unnaturalness," and, in verse 28, a desire to avoid acknowledgment of God. But although the censure fits the idolatrous people with whom Paul was concerned here, it does not seem to fit the case of a sincere homosexual Christian. Such a person loves Jesus Christ and wants above all to acknowledge God in all of life, yet for some unknown reason feels drawn to someone of the same sex, for the sake of love rather than lust. Is it fair to describe that person as lustful or desirous of forgetting God's existence?

We might think, for example, of an illustration presented by Norman Pittenger, a Cambridge theologian. Two men who had lived together devotedly and faithfully for ten years, who were known to be devout Christians, told him about their love relationship. Pittenger remarked that they had become so totally one that it seemed impossible to think of their ever separating. But what may seem shocking and even blasphemous to some Christians is that they went on to tell Pittenger that they found great joy in sexually celebrating their love on Saturday night and then kneeling side by side the next morning to take Holy Communion together.[10] Because of the training most of us have received, such a story probably sets up waves of cognitive dissonance once again. Pittenger's comment was that what these men told him was "both beautiful and right."

Possibly Pittenger's reasoning was similar to that of the Jesuit priest John McNeill, who has criticized the traditional Catholic attitude for unwittingly encouraging promiscuity:

> If a Catholic homosexual confessed occasional promiscuity, he could receive absolution and be allowed to receive communion in good conscience. If, however, he had entered into a genuine permanent love relationship, he would be judged in "a state of sin," and unless he expressed a willingness to break off that relationship he would be denied absolution.

McNeill goes on to say that the Church's attitude has "tended to undermine the development of healthy interpersonal relationships among homosexuals and gave the appearance that the Church disapproved more of the love between homosexuals than it did of their sexual activity as such."[11]

NATURAL VERSUS UNNATURAL IN ROMANS

The passage in Romans says nothing about homosexual *love.* The emphasis is entirely on sexual activity in a context of lust and idolatry. But what about the third point in this passage—doing that which, in the traditional King James wording, is "against nature"?

What seems "natural" in any culture is often simply a matter of accepted social custom; and sometimes Paul spoke of nature in that way. For example, in 1 Cor. 11:14–15, Paul raises the question, "Does not Nature herself teach you that while flowing locks disgrace a man, they are a woman's glory?" However, in Greek and Roman culture, homosexuality was at least to some extent part of accepted social custom, and no doubt it seemed as natural as anything else to many persons. Thus, in Rom. 1:26–27, it is doubtful that Paul is speaking of nature in the sense of custom, unless he is referring to a violation of Jewish custom and law. This latter possibility should not be ruled out entirely, for according to Morton Scott Enslin, the forbidden activities of Leviticus, chapter 18, "comprised *araiyot,* the third of the cardinal sins." During the days of Hadrian, a conference of rabbis decided that, because of the persecutions and the possibility of execution, a Jew might momentarily set aside any of the demands of the Torah except three. These three were that a Jew must never recognize heathenism, shed blood, nor yield to the sexual sins such as incest or homosexual acts. Enslin remarks, "This reveals the abhorrence the Jew felt at such irregularities and goes far toward explaining Paul's attitude."[12]

It is also possible that Paul had in mind the "natural" complementary design of male and female bodies, specifically their ability to fit together sexually in such a way as to produce children. Throughout church history, such so-called "natural law" arguments played an important role in shaping attitudes toward human sexuality. Are, then, certain acts in themselves unnatural? Many heterosexual couples include in their lovemaking a variety of sexual expressions in addition to coitus (penis in the vagina). Modern marriage manuals, for example, highly recommend oral-genital sex. Margaret Evening hints at a certain inconsistency in the common view held by the Christian who feels that homosexual *acts* are sinful even though the *condition* of being a homosexual is not sinful in itself. Such a person is disgusted and revolted by acts of tenderness and intimacy between homosexuals, "even though he engages in almost exactly the same love play in his own heterosexual relationships."[13]

There are other problems with the "crimes against nature" view as it is commonly held in law and theology. Enslin assumes that in order to stress the degradation to which idolatry led, Paul is saying that the heathen had sunk to the point of exchanging "the normal intercourse that animals indulge in for that actually contrary to nature."[14] A prominent evangelist reflects the same assumption when he claims that "homosexuality is a sin so rotten, so low, so dirty, that even cats and dogs don't practice it."[15] Yet modern research has shown that homosexual contact is not at all "unnatural" if we are going to use practices in the animal world as our criteria. Not only do many animals engage in same-sex relations (including mounting),[16] but among some primates the elements of same-sex affection and loyalty have also been observed.[17] Recently, researchers have even discovered "lesbian" seagulls. In a study of seagull nesting habits scientists were surprised to discover that some of the couples consisted of two females that had simply set up housekeeping together in the manner customary for male and female. They had eggs in their nests—but the eggs were usually infertile. However, there were a few cases of "bisexuality," in which a female seagull would get together with a male and produce fertile eggs, yet continue to nest with another female.[18]

THE SOCIAL CONTEXT OF ROMANS 1

Just as we have kept in mind that the Sodom story must be studied in the context of the reprehensibleness of *inhospitality* and *gang rape,* we must keep in mind that the context in chapter 1 of Romans is one of *idolatry* and *lust.* No reference is made to persons whose own "nature," or primary orientation, is homosexual, as that term is understood by behavioral scientists. What Paul seems to be emphasizing here is that persons who are heterosexual by nature have not only exchanged the true God for a false one but have also exchanged their ability to relate to the opposite sex by indulging in homosexual behavior that is not natural to them.

The homosexual practices known to Paul usually involved adultery. In Greece, it was common for a man to have a wife and also a young male lover on the side. According to James Graham-Murray, such an arrangement was considered "as a supplement to marriage recognized by the state." Male prostitution was a flourishing business on the Athens streets and in the brothels, where slave boys serviced clients, angering the city's female prostitutes, who complained about the competition.[19]

When it came to Rome, Paul was not the only one to express alarm over the emphasis on sensuality and luxury. Polybius complained of the "widespread depravity" of young Romans "since they had quickly acquired, in the war with Perseus, the moral laxity of the Greeks with regard to this kind of life." It was a sad state of affairs, he said, when young men were willing to pay "a talent for a young male lover or 300 drachmae for a jar of smoked fish from the Black Sea," and he referred to Cato's assertion that "the degeneration of the state could be seen most clearly when alluring boys were found commanding a higher price than farms, and jars of fish were worth more than plowmen."[20]

TWO PROBLEMATIC GREEK WORDS

In this kind of atmosphere, the harsh judgements of the remaining two Bible passages that deal with some type of homosexual activity, 1 Cor. 6:9–10 and 1 Tim. 1:9–10, are understandable.

> Know ye not that the unrighteous shall not inherit the kingdom of God? Be not deceived: neither fornicators, nor idolaters, nor adulterers, nor effeminate, nor abusers of themselves with mankind,

nor thieves, nor covetous, nor drunkards, nor revilers, nor extortioners, shall inherit the kingdom of God (1 Cor. 6:9–10, KJV).

Knowing this, that the law is not made for a righteous man, but
for the lawless and disobedient, for the ungodly and for sinners, for
unholy and profane, for murderers of fathers and murderers of mothers, for manslayers, for whoremongers, for them that defile themselves with mankind, for menstealers, for liars, for perjured persons,
and if there be any other thing that is contrary to sound doctrine
(1 Tim. 1:9–10, KJV).

Interpretations of these passages depend on two Greek words
used in 1 Cor. 6:9 which have presented a problem for translators.
In the King James Version, they are translated "effeminate" and
"abusers of themselves with mankind." In the Revised Standard
Version of 1952, they were combined and rendered simply
"homosexuals," which implied that all persons whose erotic interests were oriented to the same sex were by that very fact excluded
from membership in the kingdom of God. But the original intent
seems to have been to single out specific *kinds* of same-sex practices that were considered deplorable. The translators of the New
International Version capture this intent by employing the terms
male prostitutes and *homosexual offenders*. Similarly the Jerusalem Bible uses the terms *catamites* and *sodomites*. Catamites
were youths kept especially for sexual purposes; they often were
able to extort huge sums of money from the older men who were
interested in them. The second term could mean "obsessive corruptor of boys"; or it could refer to male prostitution.[21] The
Greek word translated *sodomite* is also used in 1 Tim. 1:10
("them that defile themselves with mankind," KJV).

By using these two terms, could Paul have had in mind sexual
exploitation of the kind mentioned, for example, in the first-
century manuscript *The Satyricon?* In one incident, a boy's parents had hired a trusted tutor to be the boy's constant companion

and guide, only to have their trust violated. The tutor boasted to friends that he had tricked the parents and gradually persuaded the young boy to grant him sexual favors by promising gifts of increasing value—first some doves, then a rooster, then a stallion which he was unable to deliver.[22] Petronius, the author of *The Satyricon,* was the director of court entertainment under the emperor Nero. His manuscript gives us a vivid and extremely realistic picture of the luxuries and vices of the Imperial Age.

Nero himself deserved the title, "corruptor of boys." Another first-century writer, Suetonius, who delighted in revealing gossip about the Roman rulers, had this to say about one of Nero's affairs:

> Having tried to turn the boy Sporus into a girl by castration, he went through a wedding ceremony with him—dowry, bridal veil and all —which the whole Court attended; then brought him home, and treated him as a wife. . . . A rather amusing joke is still going the rounds: the world would have been a happier place had Nero's father Domitius married that sort of wife.[23]

Although some translators have used the English word *catamite* to capture the meaning of the first of the two Greek words usually associated with homosexual practices in 1 Cor. 6:9, the Greek word literally means "soft," and is used elsewhere in the New Testament in ways that have nothing whatsoever to do with sex (for instance, in Luke 7:25 and Matt. 11:8).[24] Enslin tells us that "the uncertainty of the exact meaning of the term is as old as Dionysius of Halicarnassus (30 B.C.), who said that the tyrant Aristodemus had received the epithet either because of his effeminate practices or else because of his gentle disposition."[25] Milton may have caught the biblical meaning of the word *soft* or *effeminate,* when he applied the expression *effeminate* to males who can think about nothing but running after women, giving sexual conquest so much importance that they ignore God's will for them and thus contribute nothing to the good of humanity.[26] Since the word *effeminate* usually meant "self-indulgent" or "voluptuous" in the seventeenth century,[27] it seems probable that the King James translators meant it to convey that meaning (rather than homosexuality) in 1 Cor. 6:9. But since self-indulgence is far more widespread than homosexuality, it has perhaps been convenient to narrow the meaning of the passage so that it applies to only a scapegoat minority of the population.

LAW VERSUS GRACE

Whatever specific same-sex abuses are referred to in 1 Cor. 6:9 and 1 Tim. 1:10, an important point needs emphasis. In 1 Cor. 6:9–10 (KJV) it says that not only "effeminate" persons and "abusers of themselves with mankind" will be excluded from God's kingdom, but also "idolaters" and "covetous" persons and "revilers" and "extortioners" and several other categories of people as well. Can any member of any Christian church honestly claim that he or she is completely guiltless of idolatry? To make that claim, we would have to be living in total selflessness, without the preoccupation with the private ego (the "old nature") with which the apostle Paul wrestled all his life and with which all the rest of us must constantly wrestle as well. Repeatedly the ego usurps God's place in our minds, and repeatedly we have to turn from that idol to serve the living God. So we are all, repeatedly, idolaters.

And can any of us claim that we are not frequently guilty of covetousness, of having a craving for something we do not currently possess? And do we never revile other persons (that is, use abusive language toward them)? And how often are the corporation executives and business persons in our churches reminded that to grossly overprice their products (that is, to be extortioners) will exclude them from the kingdom of heaven? Like the first chapter of Romans, 1 Cor. 6:9–11 applies to us all.

In general terms, 1 Cor. 6:9 (KJV) tells us that "the unrighteous shall not inherit the kingdom of God." And that generalization surely includes *all* of us, unless or until by the grace of God we are washed and sanctified and justified. The point of 1 Cor. 6:9–11 is that no unrighteous person will enter the kingdom, no matter what his or her particular brand of unrighteousness may be. But some of Paul's listeners who once were unrighteous have now been washed, sanctified, and justified; they will enter the kingdom. The contrast here, in other words, is the one so often present in Paul's writings: we are unrighteous and cannot please God in our old natures, but through the acceptance of a new nature in Christ Jesus we are made fit for the kingdom. Similarly, in 1 Tim. 1:8–11 there is a contrast between condemnation of various sins under the law and the "glorious gospel of the blessed God."

When Paul says in 1 Cor. 6:11, after his list of sinners, that "such *were* some of you," he cannot mean that only *some* of his readers used to be unrighteous, for Paul is very clear about the fact that "there is none righteous, no, not one" (Rom. 3:10, KJV). He must therefore mean that only some have been washed, sanctified, and justified, while others remain in their unregenerate state. Or perhaps he means that some of his listeners had in the past been guilty of the specific *kinds* of unrightousness included in the list. But by no means can the definition of unrighteousness (and the need for grace) be limited to the specific sins mentioned. *All* of us must see ourselves included there, for we cannot doubt that we all need to be washed, sanctified, and justified in order to enter the kingdom.

Since the Greek words concerning same-sex abuses refer to specific kinds of acts rather than to the condition of being homosexual, it is improper to use 1 Cor. 6:11 as proof that conversion changes a homosexual orientation into a heterosexual one, as some groups have tried to claim. And to tell homosexuals on the basis of this passage that to enter God's kingdom they must cease to be homosexual, or at least cease expressing their homosexuality, is to place them under the law rather than under grace. Homosexuals cannot earn salvation by the sacrifice of their sexuality any more than heterosexuals can. According to the apostle Paul, only Christ's sacrifice is sufficient to put away sin. After conversion, just as the heterosexual has the old ego-nature to contend with, so does the homosexual convert retain the old ego-nature. Therefore homosexuals must certainly learn to cease from unloving abuses of sexuality, as heterosexuals must; and all of us must struggle against idolatry and other manifestations of the ego-nature. But Paul *is* telling us that *all* unrighteousness or wickedness or ego-centeredness separates us from God's presence and that inclusion comes only through acceptance of God's grace, "by the Spirit of our God."

QUESTIONS LEFT UNANSWERED IN THE BIBLE

A careful examination of what the Bible says about issues relating to homosexuality still leaves us with many unanswered questions. For one thing, the idea of a lifelong homosexual orientation or "condition" is never mentioned in the Bible. An evangelical pastor in the Netherlands, J. Rinzema, explains that "the confirmed homosexual was not recognized until roughly 1890. The Bible writers assumed that everyone was heterosexual and that in times of moral decay, some heterosexual people did some strange and unnatural things with each other."[28] Since the Bible is silent about the homosexual condition, those who want to understand it must rely on the findings of modern behavioral science research and on the testimony of those persons who are themselves homosexual.

The Bible, furthermore, does not mention the possibility of

a permanent, committed relationship of love between homosexuals analogous to heterosexual marriage. Surely, such a union is to be distinguished from the contexts we have looked at, contexts of violence, idolatry, and lust. But would such a relationship be permissible according to biblical standards? Or do theological considerations such as God's plan in creating male and female and bringing them together to be "one flesh" rule out homosexual unions entirely?

These questions, about which the Bible is silent, are stimulating a great deal of rethinking and renewed study among Christians today. A continuum of views on the homosexual issue appears to be developing. But in order to understand it fully, we need first to give attention to information provided by behavioral scientists. Then, relating that knowledge to biblical and theological considerations, we will be able to turn more intelligently to the issues confronting the age in which we live.

❦ 6. What Does Science Say?

To UNDERSTAND homosexuality, we must first know what it is. Finding an answer may be more difficult than we think! One of the foremost authorities on the subject, research psychologist Evelyn Hooker, has reviewed the various approaches of anthropologists, psychologists, sociologists, and biomedical researchers. After a thorough study, she concluded that "Who is homosexual?" and "What is homosexuality?" are very complex questions, clarification of which would be a lasting contribution to social science.[1] The very complexity of the topic provides good reason for Christians to refrain from hasty generalizations, labeling, and hysteria.

Some of the most noteworthy efforts toward solving the puzzle have been made by the Institute for Sex Research at Indiana University, popularly known as "the Kinsey Institute" (after its founder, Alfred C. Kinsey). Paul Gebhard, the Institute's present director, emphasizes that no scientific investigation can take place without a workable definition of the phenomenon being studied. His own definition of homosexual behavior is simple, pragmatic, and applicable cross-culturally. Here it is:

> We have found the most practical definition of homosexual behavior to be: physical contact between two individuals of the same gender

which both recognize as being sexual in nature and which ordinarily results in sexual arousal. Psychological homosexual response may be defined as sexual arousal from thinking of or seeing persons of the same gender.[2]

DEGREES OF HOMOSEXUALITY AND HETEROSEXUALITY

Studies conducted by the Institute for Sex Research have shown homosexuality to be a matter of degree—both in terms of *overt behavior* and in terms of *orientation*, or psychological response. Researchers have devised a scale from zero to six to locate persons on a continuum between *exclusive heterosexuality* (zero) and *exclusive homosexuality* (six). Varying degrees of heterosexuality and homosexuality characterize persons in between. For example, a person who is predominantly heterosexual but who has an incidental homosexual history would be rated one on the scale. Conversely, someone mainly homosexual but with an incidental response toward, or experience with, the opposite sex would be rated five. Midway on the continuum (rated three) are those persons whose erotic arousal and/or overt experience are equally heterosexual and homosexual.

Such ratings can be used to describe an entire life span, or they can be used in reference only to particular periods in a person's life. Transitory homosexual experience around the time of puberty, for instance, does not necessarily mean a person is "a homosexual" or that the homosexual behavior will continue into adulthood. "In terms of social and psychological significance," Gebhard stresses, such experimental behavior "is quite different from activity engaged in as an adult." Therefore, "it is not only useless, but confusing to learn that X percent of a group has had homosexual experience at some time in life—one does not know how much was confined to childhood and how much was in adult life."[3]

In other words, simple "never-ever" surveys alone tell us little about the incidence and meaning of homosexual experiences in people's lives. Furthermore, the simple heterosexual-homosexual dichotomy becomes all the more of a problem. If *any* overt homosexual experience at *any* point in life becomes the deciding factor that places an individual in the "homosexual" category, many persons would be labeled homosexual who do not fit that classification at all by any reasonable criteria. For if a person's present erotic responses and experiences are entirely heterosexual and he or she has long forgotten a few homosexual experiences at the time of approaching puberty, what sense does it make to call the person homosexual?

Suppose, however, we limit ourselves only to persons who have had overt sexual experience (not just psychological response) with persons of the same sex. We will also limit ourselves to those who have had that experience *since puberty*, because postpubertal activity is somewhat more significant than childhood activity. According to studies conducted by the Institute for Sex Research, between one-fourth and one-third of adult males and slightly more than one-tenth of adult females in the United States have had such experiences. But again, it would be erroneous to apply the label "homosexual" to all such persons, because many, mainly males, have had only incidental experience which occurred chiefly between puberty and age sixteen.[4] After such transitory adolescent experimentation, many of these persons go on to lead quite normal heterosexual lives, including marriage and children. It should be clear by now why Evelyn Hooker was accurate in her estimate of the complexity of the homosexual issue.

ORIENTATION VERSUS OVERT EXPERIENCE

This brings us to the matter of "orientation," or psychological response. The Kinsey researchers combined both experience and psychological response in their continuum ratings, because, as Gebhard points out, "most persons have the same numeral for both their psychic and overt." However, because this is not *always* the case, Gebhard now advocates a combined scoring system that can show discrepancies. For example, a rating of o/1 would tell us that a person has no conscious interest in homosexuality (rating of zero on psychological response) but is presently engaged in a small amount of homosexual activity (rating of one on behavior). Although such a case may not indicate any personality problems, "a discrepancy of two or more points indicates stress and/or emotional or social disturbance."[5]

Psychologist Alan Bell points out that it would be theoretically possible for someone to be exclusively heterosexual in activity while exclusively homosexual in feeling. (A case of psychological lesbianism illustrates the point—that is, a married woman who, during sexual relations with her husband, habitually has fantasies about being with a woman.) While many homosexual persons of both sexes are able to perform heterosexually, Bell explains that "it is a performance frequently bereft of either deep emotional satisfactions or intense sexual arousal." He cites the belief of some scholars that a person's past or present sexual *behavior* is "a poor indicator of his or her true sexual orientation." A detailed history of an individual's sexual *feelings* can tell us much more.[6]

Persons rated four or five on the Kinsey scale are considered by the Institute for Sex Research to be "predominantly homosexual." These are persons whose erotic arousal and/or overt behavior are directed more toward the same sex than toward the other sex. If we combine the predominantly homosexual with the exclusively homosexual—persons who respond *only* to the same sex (rated six)—we are able to gain some idea of the percentage of homosexuals in the United States. After taking into account the sampling problems in the original Kinsey research and also incorporating some later research, the Institute currently estimates that 4 to 5 percent of adult American males may be considered homosexual (most of this percentage is in the "exclusive" category). Among adult females, about 1 to 2 percent are predominantly or exclusively homosexual (including fours through sixes on the scale). These findings, it is interesting to note, correspond with various European studies.[7]

AN ANALOGY BETWEEN HOMOSEXUALITY AND LEFT-HANDEDNESS

For Christians who are concerned about biblical ethics, the real problems appear at this point. Nothing in the Bible deals with sexual orientation in this way. We saw that there were prohibitions about homosexual behavior in various contexts, such as idolatry, and as a violation of what was assumed to be a universally heterosexual nature in human beings. But no provision was made for persons whose "nature" itself appears to be homosexual—that small percentage of persons whose erotic response is directed toward the same sex, regardless of whether or not they ever act on that response.

A British group of Quakers saw the issue clearly when they wrote in 1963: "The word 'homosexuality' does not denote a course of conduct, but a state of affairs, the state of loving one's own, not the opposite, sex; it is a state of affairs in nature. One should no more deplore 'homosexuality' than left-handedness."[8] And in Holland, as long ago as 1949, it was suggested that the word *homophilia* be used to refer to the orientation, because the term *homosexuality* "so strongly implies the sexual act."[9]

The British group's comparison of homosexuality to left-handedness suggests that homosexuality is simply a variant of sexual expression rather than a matter of morality. Homosexuality can certainly *become* a moral matter, depending upon how it is expressed (and the same is true for the heterosexual orientation). The comparison to left-handedness also suggests that homosexuality is not a mental illness, although of course there are homosexuals with serious mental problems just as there are heterosexuals with serious mental problems.

Psychology professor John Money, a leading authority on psychosexual development, points out that "the disposition toward one sexual orientation or the other does appear to be inborn, however, as a result of the influence of sex hormones on the development of sexual pathways in the brain." He, too, uses the analogy of a person's being left-handed, ambidextrous, or right-handed. "The cause [of handedness] is not fully explainable, though there does appear to be an innate plus a learned component," he writes. "The same applies to homosexuality, bisexuality, and heterosexuality." Yet, just as schoolteachers and parents at one time punished left-handed children in efforts to force them to become right-handed, there are societal efforts to punish homosexual persons today through discriminatory practices and laws. Money calls such punishment "ineffectual" and argues that its aim is unrealistic, since forcing homosexuals to become heterosexuals is not possible, "any more than it is possible to force a heterosexual person into becoming a homosexual."[10]

A great deal of controversy has arisen among adherents of the moral, sickness, and natural variant viewpoints on homosexuality, including controversy within the religious community. Those who see homosexuality as nothing less than *sin* appeal to the biblical passages we have already examined. Those who see homosexuality as *sickness* appeal to a long tradition within the psychoanalytic school of thought.

CONTRADICTORY PSYCHOANALYTIC THEORIES

From a psychoanalytic standpoint, homosexuality is viewed by some as an arrested state of development—a failure to pass beyond a normal "homosexual stage of life" and to go on to more "mature" sexual relationships. Others argue that it is the result of an incestuous attachment to the parent of the opposite sex which creates a sense of "forbidden attraction" with regard to that sex. Conversely, some have postulated an attachment to the *same-sex* parent, with the other parent being seen as a rival, along with all other persons of the "rival's" sex. Still others suggest that the problem lies in a failure to identify with the same-sex parent. Some psychoanalytic theories relate homosexuality to castration anxieties among males; others relate it to feelings of hostility toward, or fear of, the opposite sex based on disturbed parent-child relations. According to still other theories, the choice of a same-sex love object indicates a narcissistic quest for a symbol of one's own self. Thus Wilhelm Stekel, a Viennese psychiatrist who was friend and assistant to Sigmund Freud, argued: "I believe I have proven successfully that the homosexual is a neurotic. . . . But we must not think that, like the average neurotic, the homosexual is incapable of love. Only, all his love is a love centered exclusively on self. . . . Since the homosexual loves only himself he seeks only himself in others."[11]

Many of these theories and the studies cited to support them are internally inconsistent and contradictory to one another. All are based on what has come to be called the "medical model of homosexuality"—the assumption that homosexuality is pathological, an illness in need of treatment. Sociologists Martin Weinberg and Colin Williams argue that "the emphasis on cure has often inhibited theoretical progress and a better understanding of homosexuality and the homosexual." Furthermore, many of the studies related to these theories use faulty methods "which do not measure up to minimal canons of scientific research." Many psychologists and psychiatrists have tended to base their conclusions upon small samples from among their own patients. For instance, how can Stekel honestly claim to have *proven* that "the homosex-

ual is neurotic" when the only homosexuals he had studied were
the subjects of clinical case studies? All of his evidence was drawn
from persons who felt they had serious enough problems to search
out psychiatric help! Weinberg and Williams point out that instead of claiming "by fiat" that homosexuals are maladjusted,
homosexuals *must* be studied in comparison with adequate
heterosexual control groups.[12]

INADEQUATE RESEARCH METHODS

Some theories and studies have provided the basis for sweeping assertions about homosexuality that have caused much pain
and grief—not only for homosexual persons themselves, but for
their parents as well. Fathers of homosexuals have been described
as cold and rejecting. Some studies present mothers as close-
binding but not dominant. Other researchers see mothers as dominant, strong, and controlling, while still others have presented
mothers of homosexuals as hostile and rejecting. As behavioral
scientist David Lester has noted, "It is remarkable that despite
the fact that the evidence on these points is inconsistent, the
description of the parents of the homosexual has become standardized and appears with great frequency in textbooks." Lester
considers this practice both remarkable and worrisome, since certain careful researchers have demonstrated that when certain
controls are introduced into the research methodology, *no differences have been found* between parents of homosexuals and parents of heterosexuals!

Lester is also critical of the fact that almost all studies have
been based on retrospection—on how homosexual adults remember the past, including their perceptions of how their parents
behaved toward them many years ago. The parents themselves
have not usually been studied, nor have other persons who might
be able to provide further information on the home situation.

Such oversights Lester finds "inexcusable." Furthermore, he states, "We fall too easily into the error of assuming that the parent causes the child's behavior" and ignore those studies that show how children's behavior can affect parents.[13]

Parents of homosexual persons often suffer great anguish because they have been led to believe they are to blame for their children's sexual orientation. They may even come up with evidence from the past that seems to support certain theories they have heard, even though the evidence is questionable and would have been considered insignificant under other circumstances. "I must have done *something* wrong," they reason. "If I think long and hard enough, maybe I can figure out what it was."

Such guilt on the part of parents can cause problems for researchers, as a parallel case illustrates. In 1958, research was published showing that mothers of children born with mongolism (Down's syndrome) had experienced more shocks during pregnancy than did other mothers. These results were assumed to indicate that a pregnant woman's emotional state influenced the development of this condition in her unborn child. However, an important scientific breakthrough occurred shortly after that study was published. Researchers found that Down's syndrome is associated with a chromosomal abnormality and that the earlier inference about emotional factors was wrong. "The obvious explanation for the original result," writes sociologist George W. Brown, "was that mothers of the mongol children had been searching for reasons to explain their tragedy and were likely to recall shocks or to define quite ordinary events as shocks where mothers of normal children would not. In other words, they assigned a meaning to what happened during pregnancy, *after* the birth of their child, which they would not necessarily have considered noteworthy *prior* to its birth. Such reworking of the past can obviously play havoc with aetiological studies and the example is representative of a number of problems that have to be faced."[14] (In citing this illustration, it should be noted, we are most certainly *not* suggesting that homosexuality is a mental defect to be compared with Down's syndrome, but simply that there may be parallel problems associated with research on homosexuality.)

WEAKENING OF THE THEORY THAT HOMOSEXUALITY IS AN ILLNESS

Not only has the methodology of various studies come under attack in recent years; the medical model itself has become less widely accepted. Investigations by anthropologists and sociologists have provided data that call into question certain long-held assumptions of psychotherapy. Psychologists and psychiatrists themselves have done a great deal of rethinking on the subject as a result of new research. One of the outstanding examples of such research is the work of Evelyn Hooker.

During World War II, this research psychologist from the University of Southern California at Los Angeles developed a close friendship with one of her brightest students. Over a period of time, he introduced Dr. Hooker and her husband to a number of his friends; and as a spirit of trust grew, the student revealed that he was living in a homosexual relationship, a disclosure that was quite risky at the time. His friends also told about that part of their lives, and the student begged Dr. Hooker to study the homosexuals of whom they were representative: "homosexuals who function well and don't go to psychiatrists." Busy with her laboratory studies of neurotic rats, Hooker at first refused. Besides, she wondered, how could she study people who were her friends? But the student wouldn't give up. Finally, seeing the wisdom of undertaking such a study, Hooker applied for a grant from the National Institute of Mental Health. With a matched sample of thirty homosexual men and thirty heterosexual men, none of whom were in psychiatric treatment, she conducted a series of psychological tests and then turned the tests over to skilled clinicians for analysis. These psychiatrists and psychologists were unable to tell from the test results which men were homosexual and which were heterosexual. Furthermore, the study revealed no higher degree of pathology within the homosexual group than in the heterosexual group. And there were just as many homosexual men as heterosexual men who rated *superior* in the tests. The idea that homosexuality in and of itself is a mental illness simply didn't hold up under carefully monitored study.[15]

Hooker's 1954 study, along with the earlier Kinsey studies that had shown homosexual behavior to be more prevalent than had previously been thought, provided the opening wedge for a new look at the topic. Before this time, mental health experts had considered it indisputable that homosexuality was an illness, although they differed seriously about whether or not it could be cured. Through more thorough research, the way was being cleared for interdisciplinary efforts to find answers.

REVISION BY THE AMERICAN PSYCHIATRIC ASSOCIATION

In 1967, Dr. Stanley Yolles, Director of the National Institute of Mental Health, appointed a task force made up of behavioral, medical, and social scientists "to review carefully the current state of knowledge regarding homosexuality in its mental health aspects and to make recommendations for Institute programming in this area." Evelyn Hooker chaired the task force. Its attention to the topic engendered a large amount of research which, in turn, began to have an effect on attitudes toward homosexuality. Gay activists naturally seized upon the findings and the word spread: homosexuality had been demonstrated to be not a neurosis, not destructive, but simply a sexual variation. A number of state legislatures took a new look at laws prohibiting homosexual acts, and some decriminalized sex acts between consenting adults in private. Various municipalities enacted antidiscrimination ordinances to protect the civil rights of homosexual persons. The mass media began to treat the topic in a more sympathetic light.[16] And in 1973, in a move that stunned many persons and caused considerable controversy among its own members, the American Psychiatric Association (APA) voted to remove homosexuality from its official list of mental disorders.

This was not a denial that disturbed homosexuals exist. They do exist, just as surely as heterosexuals exist who are poorly integrated into society and have various mental, emotional, and special problems. What the APA was willing to acknowledge is that there are also many *healthy* homosexuals.[17]

The Association's official news release declared that "homosexuality per se implies no impairment in judgment, stability, reliability, or general social or vocational capabilities" and should not be regarded as a psychiatric disorder, but simply as one form of sexual behavior. At the same time, the APA included under mental disorders a category called "sexual orientation disturbance," a diagnostic category for persons whose "sexual interests are directed primarily toward people of the same sex and who are either disturbed by, in conflict with, or wish to change their sexual orientation."[18] In all other cases of homosexuality, it seemed to the APA unreasonable and unfair to diagnose persons as psychologically maladjusted if: (1) they were not bothering others and were staying out of trouble with the law, (2) they were capable of earning an independent living, and (3) they were capable of forming meaningful relationships with other persons. Certainly such characteristics were to be considered signs of good mental health.[19]

In the decades since Hooker's pioneering study, various other studies of homosexuals and heterosexuals have been conducted in which the two orientations have been carefully matched against each other for adequate controls. Some have concentrated on lesbians, others on male homosexuals. Again and again, these studies have indicated that in the overall, homosexual persons are as psychologically healthy and as well integrated into society as heterosexual persons are.[20]

DAMAGE CAUSED BY SOCIAL REJECTION

But isn't this picture a bit too rosy? After all, homosexual persons are living in a hostile society and would have every reason to have psychological problems. Those homosexual men and women who seek out help toward a "cure" or a change of orientation often point out that they can no longer stand being stigmatized, discriminated against, joked and sneered about, and threatened by disclosure and even blackmail. They can no longer bear having to live two lives. The strain becomes too great, the self-hatred too strong, the anxieties too engulfing. The question is this: How anxious are those who *don't* seek out help?

Aware of such considerations, Martin Weinberg and Colin Williams conducted a large-scale cross-cultural study of nonpsychiatric male homosexuals in the United States, Denmark, and the Netherlands. Like Evelyn Hooker, these young sociologists had become interested in studying the topic after meeting a homosexual person whose very *being* served to explode the familiar stereotypes. After he had addressed the Social Problems class they were team teaching in 1966, they wrote: "His very ordinariness reduced the aura of mystery surrounding the exotic label 'homosexual'. . . . His air of well-being led us to re-evaluate our thinking." Among other concerns, Weinberg and Williams wanted to find out if homosexuals differed from the general male population with respect to self-acceptance, psychosomatic symptoms, depression, and faith in others. The researchers found little difference between the two samples in two of the categories: self-acceptance and psychosomatic symptoms. They did find, however, that those in the homosexual samples in all three societies reported less happiness and less faith in others than did those in the general male population samples. Weinberg and Williams concluded that this finding was in line with the "societal rejection theory." According to that theory, homosexual persons are forced to adjust to varying degrees of legal repression and social rejection that affect personal happiness and trust—even though at the same time they may be able to adapt in such a way as to maintain a positive self-image and avoid psychosomatic symptoms.[21]

The Weinberg-Williams study suggests that the "homosexual problem" may really be a "heterosexual problem" in that society has refused to grant full human acceptance to homosexual persons. Because the "black problem" is really a problem of white racism, blacks cannot be expected to solve racial tensions on their own. Similarly, homosexuals by themselves cannot change the social pressures that have made personal trust and happiness more difficult for them to achieve than for heterosexual persons.

HEALTHY HOMOSEXUALS AND HEALTHY TRUTHFULNESS

One final study should be mentioned, since it provides some answers about different categories of homosexuals and gives us some clues about why clinical studies have failed to provide the whole picture. Aware that many studies of homosexual persons have been concerned either with psychiatric patients or with persons who were referred for treatment after being in trouble with the law, British sociologist Michael Schofield decided to explore whether or not these two groups differed from homosexuals who had never been in therapy and had never been convicted of homosexual offenses. He found that the men who had never been arrested and had never been in therapy were better integrated into the larger community in both work and leisure activities. They were more likely to be living in long-standing, stable relationships, and they were far less promiscuous than either the prison sample or the patient sample.[22] If only the findings on the patient and prison samples had been reported and then generalized as though they applied to *all* homosexuals, the third group (the healthiest group) would have been completely misrepresented. Yet this was the common practice in older studies.

An awareness of behavioral science research on homosexuality can help us as Christians to better understand and deal with questions surrounding the topic, and it is important that we avail ourselves of such knowledge as much as possible. Otherwise, it is all too easy to perpetuate old myths and stereotypes and thus to bear false witness against our neighbor.

❦ 7. From Homophobia to Understanding

To EFFECTIVELY minister to homosexual persons, Christians not only need to give serious attention to the findings of the social and behavioral sciences; we need also to face up to a number of specific issues relating to the topic. First, we must deal with the fear the subject tends to generate—what psychologist George Weinberg calls *homophobia*. [1] Second, we need to develop an understanding of the gay community. And third, we must ask ourselves if there needs to be a rethinking of homosexuality in biblical perspective. Or should we be content to rest on past approaches to the topic?

SOME FORMS OF HOMOPHOBIA

When a gay activist organization announced an "If You Are Gay, Wear Blue Jeans Today" campaign at the University of Illinois (Champaign), large numbers of students left their usual denim attire in the closet and wore dresses, skirts, slacks, and shorts. Some who inadvertently wore blue jeans went back to their rooms and changed clothes after other students made remarks or asked questions. The gay organization felt it had made its point: many people were actually afraid to wear jeans; they preferred to give up their customary attire rather than be suspected of homo-sexuality.[2]

Homophobia may take many forms: fear of being thought homosexual by others, fear of possible homosexual response in oneself, fear of "catching" homosexuality (as though it were a contagious disease), fear that children will see homosexuality as a viable alternative to heterosexual marriage and will choose a homosexual lifestyle, and so on.

Among persons who are aware that their own tendencies *are* homosexual, homophobia often takes the form of self-loathing.[3] We have already encountered a clear example of this in Dr. Howard Brown's description of his feelings as an adolescent. In another case, a lesbian Christian reports that when she was in high school and so dedicated to Christ that she resolutely avoided masturbation or any other sexual expression, the awareness of her lesbian impulses often made her afraid to get into bed. She spent hours alone in suicidal depressions because Christian leaders re-peatedly told her that God had no use for homosexuals like her-self. And author Jeremy Seabrook recalls thinking in his youth that he was "the most monstrously perverted creature on earth." He points out that when people become aware of their orienta-tion, because the word *homosexual* conjures up a certain stereo-typed image, the term "has a repelling and contaminating power which makes people recoil and say, 'That can't be me'."[4]

DISTORTIONS CAUSED BY HOMOPHOBIA

Many Christians think of homosexuality as topping the list in a hierarchy of sins. For that reason, homophobia may even result in a strange kind of "situation ethic," although that term would probably not be used. For example, one military chaplain with an evangelical affiliation reported to a civilian pastor friend that during overseas service he had encouraged the men in his charge

to visit prostitutes in what was known as the local "meat market."
When the pastor asked why he had given such advice, the chaplain replied simply, "To prevent perversion." Somehow it didn't occur to him that to use and exploit women in this way might in itself be a perversion of God's plan for sexuality. The chaplain's sole concern was to prevent homosexual acts, and to further this goal, even sex with a prostitute was considered acceptable, since at least it was heterosexual.

Homophobia can also hinder or block even supposedly objective scientific research on homosexuality. For instance, when the Institute for Sex Research made plans for its investigation of homosexuality in the 1970s, only the National Institute of Mental Health was willing to grant funds. Other sources of funding "lacked the courage to fund a large-scale objective study of homosexuality."[5] Similarly, up until very recently, homophobia has had a restraining effect on public dissemination of knowledge about homosexuality, at least in the popular media. Certain beliefs about homosexual persons were perpetuated even if it meant deliberate denial of evidence to the contrary. Psychotherapist C. A. Tripp reports that a 1967 television documentary was purposely distorted when network officials felt that the program in its original, accurate version seemed "too supportive" of homosexuals and might antagonize an important segment of the viewing public. The interviews with "happy" homosexuals seemed so positive that they outweighed the "unhappy" examples. Careful editing and cutting of the sound track changed some of the content so drastically that one man threatened to sue the network and another entered a formal complaint of fraud and withdrew his release, thereby denying the network any future reruns.

As another manifestation of homophobia, Tripp cites examples of high-ranking homosexuals (in fields such as politics and religion) who sometimes engineer moral crusades against homosexuality and seek the prosecution of known homosexual persons. "The psychology of a high-ranking homosexual's antihomosexuality can be quite complex," explains Tripp. "Although he sometimes seems motivated by a simple desire to protect his own position, he more often exercises a complicated morality in which he justifies his own preferences by publicly attacking nearby variations as outrageous."[6] We are reminded of Christ's illustration of hypocrisy: seeking to remove the mote (a splinter of wood) from the eye of someone else before removing the beam (a large 2 × 4) from one's own. And we feel sure that the Christian community would be shocked indeed to learn that some of the most repeated attacks on homosexuality are coming from people who themselves engage secretly in homosexual practices. Of course, Tripp does not say, and we are not implying, that *all* moral crusades against homosexuality are conducted by persons who are themselves homosexual. Yet, as Dr. Richard Green points out, in any case of very strong anti-homosexual feelings, one may suspect "conflict at some level."[7]

IS HOMOSEXUALITY ON THE INCREASE?

Other ways homophobia manifests itself are connected with the frequent assertions that homosexuality is on the increase and that if nothing is done to stop it, more and more people will choose to become homosexual. For one thing, these assertions betray a deep lack of faith in the attractions of heterosexuality. For another, there is no reliable evidence to support the assertion that sexual orientation is simply a matter of choice. If it were, why would there be so many homosexuals in a society that rejects and punishes homosexuality?

Above all, there is no reliable evidence to support the declaration that homosexuality is on the increase. Rather, as Evelyn Hooker explains, the social *visibility* of openly declared homosexuals, the emergent homosexual organizations protesting public policy, and the widespread discussion of scientific research on the subject may make it *seem* that more homosexuality exists than ever before.[8] The evident increase, however, is in openness rather than in incidence. There is certainly no basis for the unexplained claim of one Christian author that "the incidence of male homosexuality has increased enormously—perhaps a hundred times—with the introduction of oral contraceptives"![9] Nor is there foundation for the claim of another Christian writer that "homosexuality is on the rise in today's society. And with the Women's Liberation Movement, more and more weak men are feeling threatened by women and choosing homosexual rather than heterosexual relationships."[10]

The latter statement is indicative of the homophobic reactions of some Christians to changing attitudes toward gender roles in contemporary society. In 1975, for instance, national attention was drawn to the efforts of two independent Baptist ministers in New Milford, Connecticut, who threatened to go to court because sixth grade children of both sexes were being required to take one-half year each of home economics and industrial arts. The ministers feared that the children—especially the boys—would become homosexuals if the schools didn't stick to traditional gender-based activities, the girls learning to cook and sew while the boys learned metalworking and carpentry.[11]

In a similar vein, a book on Christian child rearing contains a section on "how to develop your normal child into a homosexual." High on the list of warnings for parents of boys is this: "Teach him to sew and cook, and how to knit, too. After all, sexist attitudes about chores are out of date nowadays." Quoting 1 Cor. 6:9–10, the same author goes on to say, "Here God makes it quite plain that even being an effeminate boy is sin in His sight."[12] Think of the damage such statements can do to a boy or young man of a gentle, sensitive, artistic or poetic bent—or to a young man who, for hormonal reasons or because of certain chromosomal irregularities is considered "effeminate" in physical appearance. Such a person is being told that his very *being* is sin!

THREE COMPONENTS OF SEXUAL IDENTITY

Part of the confusion and fear about homosexuality is related to a failure to distinguish among three components of sexual identity. As psychiatry professor Richard Green has noted, these components involve: (1) our basic conceptions of ourselves as being either male or female (our gender identities), (2) how we conform to expected behavior for our sex as defined by our particular culture (our gender roles), and (3) whether, in terms of a sexual partner, we are attracted to someone of the same or the opposite sex (our sexual orientation).[13]

Gender roles (number two on the above list) vary from culture to culture and are undergoing extensive rethinking and change in our own culture. Thus, males may feel more free to be tender and to participate in activities traditionally thought "feminine," whereas females may feel more free to be assertive and to participate in work and activities traditionally considered "masculine." In such cases, persons are following *individual* interests, abilities, and personality, instead of trying to fit into a mold determined solely by their having been born into a *category* of male or female.

A person may not conform to gender-role stereotypes and yet have a "gender identity" or self-concept (number one in the above list) that matches his or her anatomy. Even though he may be knitting a sweater at the moment, the male thinks, "I am a boy," or "I am a man." Even though she may be in athletic events or in law school, the female thinks, "I am a girl," or "I am a woman." This is in contrast to the thinking of the *transsexual* who considers himself or herself to be a member of the opposite sex trapped in the "wrong body," and who may even seek hormonal treatment and sex reassignment through surgery.[14] It should also be noted that a person who doesn't conform to gender-role stereotypes is not necessarily attracted to persons of the same sex (number three on the list). Some homosexuals do not fulfill traditional gender-role expectations, but many do. In others words, many lesbians look and act extremely "feminine," and many male homosexuals look and act extremely "masculine." In the same way, heterosexuals may take on either traditional or nontraditional gender roles. Thus, taken by itself, number two on Green's list (gender roles) must not be confused with either number one (which may relate to transsexualism) or number three (which may relate to homosexuality). Confusing these three components of sexual identity can only serve to divide, distress, and misinform the Christian community.

HOMOSEXUALITY—OR FRIENDSHIP?

Another area of homophobia that we Christians must face is our fear and suspicion about close same-sex friendships. How can we expect the world to "know that we are Christ's disciples by our love for one another" if we're *afraid* to love each other because somebody might think we're homosexual? Persons who are basically heterosexual need to realize that affectionate feelings toward friends of the same sex do not necessarily entail *erotic* feelings. There is no reason, because of simply feeling affection, to fear that one is somehow "becoming" homosexual. It is certainly possible to feel and speak of love for someone else without the slightest desire to express that love through genital sexual relations. Shakespeare was affirming exactly that sort of close friendship when he wrote, "Let me not to the marriage of true *minds* / Admit impediments."[15] In his anthropological study *Friends and Lovers,* Robert Brain writes that "Friendship need not derive from an unconscious sexual drive but a cultural imperative to exchange ideas, sentiments, and goods. . . . To me, it is the strangest thing that in Western Christian society, founded on the love of God and the fellowship of mankind, loneliness has become one of the hallmarks."[16]

In a world yearning for intimacy, we need to rid ourselves of the fears that keep us from knowing the depth of friendship displayed in such biblical examples as Ruth and Naomi or David and Jonathan. We are denying ourselves choice gifts of God if we let homophobia rob us of the joy of telling friends we love them and hearing them speak of their love for us, or of holding a friend who needs a shoulder to cry on, or of clasping a hand to show we care, or of hugging in a way that simply expresses a sense of affection and kinship.[17] Similarly, we need to take care that we do not attribute homosexuality to others simply because we observe a deep and close relationship or see two persons of the same sex sharing a home. They may or may not be homosexual, but it is not our business to judge, and suspicions are often unfounded. Needless gossip has caused a great deal of discomfort and pain to single persons who greatly need warm, intimate relationships and a sense of family. In this regard, the Kinsey researchers showed great sensitivity by taking into consideration the human tendency toward suspicion and gossip. "It should be emphasized," they wrote, "that a high proportion of unmarried females who live together never have contacts which are in any sense sexual."[18]

HOMOSEXUALS AND CHILDREN

One last way that homophobia manifests itself is through the belief that homosexuals are out to catch small children, either for purposes of recruitment into the gay lifestyle or for purposes of seduction and even rape. The "recruitment" idea received national publicity during the campaign that defeated the anti-discrimination ordinance in Dade County, Florida. Because homosexuals are biologically unable to reproduce themselves, it was argued, they seek to grow in numbers through recruiting other people's children.[19] Such an assertion involves gross factual distortion and a lack of understanding of the multiple factors which contribute to a person's becoming homosexual. People cannot simply be "recruited" into homosexuality. The propensity is already there at a very early age. It is apparently the result of a complex interaction of influences not yet fully understood, which may include both genetic/biological factors and social/psychological factors.[20]

"Think of the efforts that have been made through the ages by heterosexuals to seduce homosexuals," argues Dr. Mary Calderone of the Sex Information and Education Council of the U.S. "It doesn't work either way." She stresses a need to view sexual orientation, whether heterosexual or homosexual, not in terms of sexual acts but as a state of being. "Furthermore," she writes, "no one who was programmed by five years of age to be heterosexual can be seduced to become homosexual, any more than the reverse."[21]

The stereotype of the homosexual child-seducer has arisen from sensationalized media reports of isolated instances in which a school teacher, scout worker, camp or club leader is arrested for sexual activities (perhaps even rape) of young boys. An example is the case of the grisly sex-torture, mass murders that took place around Houston, Texas several years ago. Over a period of time, many teenage runaway boys were lured into a sadistic sexual situation and then killed. Such cases, however, are in a category by themselves. The fact that homosexual acts took place should not make us think of such disturbed men as representative of homosexuals in general, any more than we would want to think of rapists or molesters of little girls as being representative of heterosexuals in general.

In fact, according to Alan Bell of the Institute for Sex Research at Indiana University, child-seduction and child-molestation are usually heterosexual phenomena. Most of us remain unaware of this because when media reports are released concerning male attacks on girls or women, the word *heterosexual* is never used, whereas releases concerning male attacks on boys invariably use the word *homosexual.* Hence, we are lured into the false assumption that homosexual offenses are more common than heterosexual ones.

Bell reports that the Institute's data show that almost never did homosexual males report being introduced to homosexuality during childhood through seduction by older males.[22] On a similar note, sociologists William Simon and John Gagnon have written that, contrary to popular stereotypes, seduction by an older woman does not appear to be a common "mode of entry into homosexuality" for most lesbians.[23]

There is, of course no denying that child seduction (both heterosexual and homosexual) does exist. Parents should certainly teach their children how to recognize and cope with sexual invitations and sexual overtures on the part of adults. *Pederasts* (men who are erotically attracted to young boys) are not necessarily exclusively or primarily homosexual; they may be married and sexually active with their wives and may even have children of their own. Sometimes they are just as sexually attracted to young girls, and thus might more accurately be termed *pedophiliacs* (adults who desire sexual relationships with children under the age of puberty).[24] In general, most homosexuals (like most heterosexuals) are sexually attracted to adults, not to children. Perhaps it is wise to keep *pedophiliacs* or *pedarasts* from teaching children. But from the standpoint of the children's safety, there is no more reason for barring an ordinary homosexual from working with children than there is for barring an ordinary heterosexual from the same job.

HOMOSEXUALS AS ROLE MODELS

This still leaves us with the issue of homosexuals as role models in society and especially in the schools. A guest editorial in the *Christian Century* states the problem as it is perceived by many thinking Christians: "Children become adults and take their places in society by patterning their behavior after role models. . . . It is inescapable: sanctioning homosexual life-styles will affect the way the young perceive adult society, and it will have an effect on the kind of people they grow up to be."[25] According to this line of thought, for a school board to hire a known homosexual would constitute social sanction of homosexuality. And the more effective and popular the homosexual teacher turned out to be in the classroom and larger school community, the more dangerous that teacher's influence would be. Such reasoning no doubt undergirded the outcome of a June, 1977, Gallup poll which indicated that although 56 percent of Americans generally favor equal job opportunities for homosexuals, only 27 percent expressed a willingness for homosexual persons to be hired as elementary school teachers.[26]

Fears about homosexuals as role models, either inside or outside the schools, are based on the assumption that homosexuality is a matter of choice. But Dr. Paul Gebhard, director of Indiana University's Institute for Sex Research, states that he has never known of anyone who is homosexual by choice. The only choice possible is whether or not to *accept* one's homosexuality. We saw in chapter 6 that there are many contradictory theories about the origins of homosexuality. Dr. Gebhard stresses that the factors leading to homosexuality are extremely complex, while the orientation is not a matter of conscious choice.[27]

Dr. Anke Ehrhardt, a leading researcher in gender identity, sex differences, and sexual orientation, agrees. She comments that "homosexuality is still a phenomenon that we cannot really explain. Not only is the research inconclusive as far as hormones are concerned, but as far as environmental learning factors are concerned." She points out that in her current research on lesbians, no one factor seems to predict the development of the homosexual orientation. There was nothing unusual about the parental background of the women in her sample, and in fact the sample showed an unusually low percentage of divorced homes.[28] Since parents form the first and frequently the most influential role models, it is important to remember that most homosexuals were brought up by heterosexual parents!

The converse also seems to be true: children reared by homosexual parents are turning out to be heterosexual. In his ongoing longitudinal studies of children who are pre-transsexual or pre-homosexual, Richard Green has found that their parents are thoroughly unremarkable on attitude scales and clinical tests. And at the same time, in his studies of children being reared by male-to-female and female-to-male transsexuals, and by lesbian couples, the children are thus far all developing as heterosexuals. These children are in all respects typical children. Nothing remarkable has shown up at all. This has led Dr. Green to conclude that "maybe parents don't have a lot to do with the sex typing of children."[29] His findings provide a whole new dimension for reasoning about role models: parents are the first and most intimate role models a child knows, and "atypical" children are being brought up by "typical" parents, while "typical" children are being brought up by "atypical" parents! One conclusion seems clear: close proximity to adults of either homosexual or heterosexual persuasion does not in itself cause children to become either homosexual or heterosexual.

A number of researchers are convinced that there is an interaction between neuroendocrine factors and social learning, not yet fully understood, that may predispose persons toward homo-sexuality or transsexualism.[30] Psychology professor Heino Meyer-Bahlburg has explained that we have, to date, "very little knowl-edge of sexual orientation in general," including heterosexual orientation. "What we need are prognostic longitudinal develop-mental studies that will have to take into account sex-dimorphic behavior in general, peer-group socialization, and pubertal matu-ration. When we are able to identify the factors that contribute to the development of heterosexual orientation, then we will probably be able to delineate those which lead to homosexual development." Meyer-Bahlburg goes on to speculate that perhaps in human beings "endocrine factors contribute to the develop-ment of sexual orientation by way of facilitation of specific sexual learning."[31] Alertness to the great complexity of factors involved in the development of homosexuality has prompted Dr. Alan Bell and his associates to undertake one of the largest studies of homo-sexual life-styles ever attempted. The second volume will carry the revealing title of *Sexual Orientation: Its Multiple Roots and Ori-gins.*

As we have just seen, Professor Meyer-Bahlburg writes of the need for longitudinal developmental studies. Because the longitu-dinal studies already underway have uncovered no evidence that adult role models influence a child's sexual orientation, we can begin to understand why four psychiatrists recently felt free to issue a joint public statement that "homosexuals as 'role models' do not influence children's sexual orientation."[32]

There is no question that teachers influence their students for better or worse in those areas where the students are able to exercise choice. Since basic sexual orientation is not one of those areas, the hiring of homosexuals in the schools is best approached as the kind of issue it really is: an issue of civil rights. Here the fairest and most responsible approach would seem to be a *single standard* for both heterosexual and homosexual persons. For instance, if a heterosexual teacher began to tell her grade school class about what goes on between her and her husband in the privacy of their bedroom, she would very quickly be dismissed for conduct unbecoming a faculty member. The same standard would certainly apply to a homosexual teacher. If a heterosexual wrote on his job application or stated in his interview that he was enthusiastic about oral-genital sex or some other heterosexual variation, the school board would probably not hire him because of his lack of discretion. They would probably react the same way to a homosexual person who announced his or her homosexuality on the application or during the interview. Their reason would quite possibly be the same—disturbance at the lack of discretion —and homosexuals should not be too quick to charge antihomosexual bias.

On the other hand, school boards would not investigate whether or not an applicant presumed to be heterosexual had, for example, ever engaged in oral-genital sex or other heterosexual variations, nor would they try to find out whether the fraternity or sorority listed on the application had a reputation for wild parties or for showing pornographic films. The same standard should apply to those applicants presumed to be homosexual. In other words, as far as jobs are concerned—including teaching jobs —the sexual orientation and behavior of any individual should be irrelevant as long as it is reasonably private, and unless actual performance on the job can be shown to be negatively affected. Teacher-training courses have always emphasized the importance of teacher behavior as a possible influence on the young, not only in the classroom but also in the surrounding community. Perhaps such courses should properly include discussion of the professional risks involved in public labeling of one's sexual orientation and behavior. Is it really anybody else's concern?

Russell Baker reminisces in the *New York Times Magazine* that at least two of his high school teachers were homosexuals. One of them, he remembers, had encouraged a classmate to become proficient in an art for which he is now world-renowned, and did so without affecting the classmate's heterosexual orientation. The other taught Baker himself that life can be witty—and wit is the hallmark of Baker's success—without affecting Baker's enthusiastic heterosexuality. Beneath his grin, Baker supplies an important corrective to the fear that the homosexual life style will be copied by students: "If the teacher was a 'role model,' parents were obviously unaware of it, for most of them surely did not want their children to grow up to be spinsters. Yet, despite almost constant tutelage by spinsters, I never felt the slightest temptation to indulge in spinsterism."[33]

First-rate teachers, whether heterosexual or homosexual, can provide valuable role models in effective use of language, in attitudes of compassion and social concern, in disciplined work habits, in graceful behavior under stress, in love of life and learning, and the like.[34] (In fact, good homosexual teachers have been doing exactly those things for many years. Their homosexuality is unknown for two reasons: because of society's desire not to know and because of their personal belief that their sexual orientation is nobody's business but their own.)

While few grade school students are aware of the sexual orientation of their teachers, junior high and high school students are given to such speculation, often very acute and accurate speculation. For a student who knows that he or she is developing in a homosexual direction—frequently a terrifying and guilt-ridden secret—becoming aware that a certain admired teacher is homosexual could have extremely positive results. The young person would see in that teacher the possibility of a self-accepting rather than a self-hating attitude, and might realize that it is possible for homosexuals to contribute something valuable to the world and to relate constructively to other persons. Such a young person might thus be spared a painful and destructive involvement in the promiscuity of the gay bar and bath scene, or spared from entering into heterosexual marriage in the mistaken hope that it will "cure" his or her predisposition toward homosexuality.

Psychoanalyst Theodore Isaac Rubin has argued that "any relationship, professional or otherwise, that ultimately reduces self-hate and enhances compassion contributes to a long term and possibly permanent therapeutic effect. This process in turn makes self-growth, creativity and constructive relating possible. We invariably relate better to other people when we relate better to ourselves."[35] Surely we would not want to deny the opportunity for self-acceptance and creative living to our neighbor, the homosexual!

WHAT DOES GAY MEAN?

As we pointed out in chapter 4, one of the biggest reasons for widespread homophobia is the wide gap, or social distance, heterosexual persons maintain between themselves and the homosexual world. Not knowing homosexuals as persons, many Christians can think only in terms of a category to be feared and held in disdain. Naturally, effective ministry is blocked by such an attitude. And one term especially repulsive to many Christians is the term *gay* as it is used by homosexuals about themselves.

There are a number of different theories about the origin of the specialized use of the word *gay* as an adjective or noun meaning "homosexual." But there is agreement that it served originally as a code word for secret communication among homosexual persons who felt the necessity of keeping their identity hidden from a hostile society. *Gay* means "happy," and with the growth of the homosexual liberation movement and the movement toward gay pride, many homosexual persons prefer to use that term almost exclusively. The term *gay* deliberately provides a counter image to prevailing stereotypes of the neurotic, maladjusted, unhappy homosexual. It is intended to convey a sense of self-acceptance and of high self-esteem.[36] "I'm gay and I'm proud" and "Gay is good" have become familiar slogans in the homosexual subculture.

Christians who are accustomed to thinking only in terms of "Gay is sin" are likely to reject out of hand—or even fail to hear —what the gay community is trying to say. "Gay is proud" seems to go against all we've ever been taught about homosexuality; it seems a deliberate flaunting of disobedience to God. Consequently, we may close our minds, our ears, our hearts. But for members of the gay community, "Gay is proud" is an effort to say: "I am a person, a human being, just as you are. Recognize me. Accept me. I have my share of talents. I have contributions to offer the society that is rejecting me. I am learning what it means to be accepted by others who are like me and understand me and who have helped me to see that I am not alone. I am learning to accept myself. But can you—will you—accept me?"

WHAT IS THE GAY COMMUNITY?

The gay community is not a particular geographical location, but rather an aggregate of persons, places, and activities. Members of the gay community share a sense of "socio-psychological unity" and common interests stemming from their sexual preference and the societal reaction to that preference. Through getting together and through information networks and publications, gay persons find collective support and acceptance.[37]

Actually, it is misleading to speak of the gay community as though it were some sort of monolithic institution composed of a homogeneous population. Perhaps it would be better to speak in the plural: gay communities or homosexual subcultures. What these communities have in common is their members' sense of being an oppressed minority. They seek a social life together and support from one another to help them cope in a society that stigmatizes them. But beyond that, there are enormous variations in the "gay worlds" within the larger gay world.

Perhaps the biggest distinction that needs to be made is between the public (and often more sensational) gay world and the quiet, invisible world of homosexual friendships and networks. The more public gay world includes persons who are open about their homosexuality and active in the gay movement, working for changes in laws, public attitudes, and so on. But there is another dimension of the public gay world that consists of settings conducive not only to social activities but also to initiating sexual contacts. From the standpoint of Christian ethics, the depersonalized sexual encounters of "cruising" (looking for partners solely for casual sexual contact) have elicited some of the strongest arguments to condemn the "gay lifestyle." But it is only fair to point out that, according to Laud Humphreys's important study, 54 percent of males who frequent public men's rooms for sex are married and otherwise respectable, often church and community leaders. They are seeking impersonal sex because that least jeopardizes their family and job connections and their standing in the community.[38]

Perhaps the heterosexual world should ponder its own share of responsibility for the cruising scene. In one university town, after same-sex dancing was prohibited at a favorite student gathering place, one young man expressed his disappointment in a letter to the local newspaper. "Why does society persist in forcing gays into strictly sexual situations?" he asked. "By not allowing gay people to participate in healthy social activities, society is forcing us into the bedroom, or the bar-room, and even into the restrooms; while everyone else is allowed to socialize freely and display affection in countless ways that would indeed be considered sexual were it performed by a same-sex couple."[39] What many Christians fail to realize is that many people who are cruising are searching for something much more meaningful than casual sex. Many yearn for a life-partner, even though they may be too confused and frightened to know how to sustain a long-term relationship and thus drift in and out of casual sexual encounters. "Where else can we go?" some ask. Whereas a Christian heterosexual can find a life partner at church or college socials, the homosexual often feels forced to slip off to the big city to seek out homosexual bars, even if he or she is extremely uncomfortable in that setting.

Even those who are already settled in permanent committed homosexual relationships may occasionally visit the bars, but not for reasons related to cruising. Rather, they long for a sense of social acceptance as a couple, something denied them in society at large. "It is impossible to know to what extent love is strengthened by being public," writes Dennis Altman, "yet romantic ideals of secret love notwithstanding, I suspect that after a time lovers have a real psychological need for the support that comes from being recognized as such. . . . the very concealment of love tends in time to produce strains a more open relationship could better handle."[40] Could the church, by not providing social acceptance to homosexual persons, be forcing them to rely on the limited resources of the gay communities?

Cruising for casual sex is chiefly a male phenomenon. In the most recent study by the Institute for Sex Research, only 15 percent of lesbians reported cruising, as compared to 85 percent of male homosexuals.[41] As Bell points out, "the highly charged sexual atmosphere of the gay world conspires against sexual monogamy."[42] In describing the situation, Evelyn Hooker writes, "A standardized and essential feature of interaction in bars, baths, streets, and parks is the expectation that sex can be had without obligation or commitment. Sexuality is separated from affectional and social life and is characterized by promiscuity, instrumentality, and anonymity."[43]

. PROMISCUITY AND THE "EX-GAY" MINISTRIES

Dr. Ralph Blair, a psychotherapist who directs New York's Homosexual Community Counseling Center, explains that cruising and promiscuity are not so much expressions of the sex drive as they are the futile attempts of persons with low self-esteem to find ego-stroking and self-acceptance. As a counselor and an evangelical Christian, Dr. Blair is cognizant of the various "ex-gay" ministries which claim that Christ can and does "cure" the homosexuality of those who seek healing. He has talked with some leaders of such organizations who have admitted in private (but never in public) that their own desires are as homosexual as they ever were. At least one of these ex-gay leaders still actively engages in homosexual practices. Another privately admits that he is misleading people who expect his ministry to change them into heterosexuals, only to find that the "liberation" or "deliverance" they have been promised is simply a desperate day-by-day struggle against sexual expression.

Undoubtedly, however, there are some sincere Christians who believe that they have been cured from homosexuality. We do not wish in any way to question the sincerity of these persons. Some of them may have been true bisexuals (number three on the continuum described in chapter Six). Others may have been predominantly heterosexuals who were indulging in homosexual practices as a matter of choice (ones and twos on the continuum). In either case, it is understandable that through Christ's power these persons have returned to a sexual expression that satisfies social norms without violating their own true nature. But what about people who are predominantly or exclusively homosexual (fours through sixes on the continuum)? Dr. Blair, who through counseling has helped hundreds of homosexuals overcome their need for promiscuity, explained to us by letter what may be occurring in the lives of these Christians:

> As people begin to see that they can associate with others on a basis that is not just genital, either with others who are "getting their heads together" through therapy or with other believers in Christian fellowship, they are opened up to much more meaningful interaction then they have known before. It is easy to misunderstand these newer experiences as evidence of a diminishing homosexuality. Actually it is a diminishing of the use of sex for non-sexual [self-esteem] purposes. Sooner or later, the person realizes that the authentic homosexual orientation remains intact. Sex can now be something to use . . . as an expression of affection and no longer as an inadequate means for self-acceptance.

As founder of Evangelicals Concerned, a national task force of heterosexual and homosexual Christians, Dr. Blair has heard from many persons who once sincerely thought they had been cured and who later discovered that their orientation had not in fact changed. His hope is that Evangelicals Concerned will provide for such people a place to find Christ's acceptance and also a place for working out a responsible ethic for homosexual Christians.

THE PRIVATE, ORDINARY HOMOSEXUAL COMMUNITY

There is another gay world of which Christians need to be aware: the private homosexual world made up of persons who go about their daily lives, employment, and religious and social activities just as heterosexuals do. Sex is only a small aspect of their lives and is likely to be confined to one partner in a context not unlike heterosexual marriage. Thus, Hooker is careful to draw attention to those sectors of the homosexual community where "sexuality is integrated in the affectional, personal, and social patterns of individuals who establish relatively stable and long-lasting relationships." In this invisible gay world, contrasting dramatically with the cruising of the "baths and bar scene," social occasions are apt to consist of a gathering of friends (often homosexual couples in one another's homes) for dinners, picnics, birthday celebrations, holidays, anniversaries, and so on.[44] The emphasis is social, not sexual.

Perhaps it is lack of awareness of the very *ordinariness* of everyday life in the vast hidden homosexual world that accounts for the insensitivity shown by some well-meaning Christians in their zealous opposition to gay civil rights or in their efforts to break up social relationships. After the dean of a Christian college had expelled a young homosexual and advised him to break off all contact with the homosexual community, the young man exclaimed, "But these people are my *friends!* They are very nice people! Why must I cut myself off from them when I really like them?" To a counselor he later said: "Where else can I go? Those are the people who understand me and accept me. They're interesting people who have taught me all sorts of things about art and music. So *much* of what we do has nothing at all to do with sex."[45]

Yet many Christians fail to be sensitive on this point in their warnings to "avoid contact with all former homosexual friends" and to "avoid places where such people gather."[46] Sometimes this insensitivity extends even to the terminology they use, as in this statement by a prominent theologian: "The church of Christ must never forget that the homosexual has little disposition to seek help while he associates only with his 'queer' cohorts."[47] We need to move out of such homophobia and into an understanding of why gay communities exist and what they're really like.

✿ 8. The Debate in American Christendom

HOWARD BROWN writes of a Baptist minister's son in a small midwestern town. Upon finding out that his son was homosexual, the minister told him daily that he would go to hell for committing an abomination. During the boy's senior year in high school, his father ordered him to eat his meals in his room, away from the rest of the family. Although he was an outstanding musician and had won state and national music contests, he was told that he could not play the church piano and, indeed, was not to attend the church at all. On graduation day, the father sent the boy's brothers and sisters out of the house and handed the young man his "gift." It was an envelope containing twenty-five dollars and a one-way train ticket to New York. His mother was sad, but could only say that she thought it was "best for the family."[1] In another case described by Dr. Brown, a mother put her arm around her son's shoulders after learning that he was homosexual —which he took to be a sign that she was going to accept him. Then she spoke, saying that she had made only one mistake in her life. "What do you mean?" he asked, whereupon his mother told him that she should have had an abortion twenty-two years earlier. Since that time she has been telling everyone that her son is dead.[2]

Rick Huskey, the young, former Methodist deacon mentioned in chapter 3, fared better. His parents were stunned by the disclosure of his homosexuality, but they lovingly accepted him and have stood by him ever since. Willing to share their story with the readers of a Christian family magazine, the Huskeys told a free-lance writer that "fear of rejection kept them from asking for help from the church." They felt that on the topic of homosexuality the church was playing the role of follower rather than leader, "following popular opinion instead of leading toward compassion and acceptance."[3]

RETHINKING: WORLDLY COMPROMISE OR CHRISTLIKE LEADERSHIP?

Yet some Christians would argue that any trend toward acceptance of homosexuality *is* following popular opinion, rather than standing fast on Christian principles that condemn homosexual practices. As we have seen, the Bible clearly condemns certain kinds of homosexual practices (in the context of gang rape, idolatry, and lustful promiscuity). However, it appears to be silent on certain other aspects of homosexuality—namely, the matter of a homosexual orientation as described by modern behavioral sciences and also the matter of a committed love relationship analogous to heterosexual monogamy. Realization of these gaps in biblical teaching constitutes the basic reason that many Christians are reconsidering the subject. This rethinking has been given added impetus by the growing awareness of personal incidents such as those described in the first section of this chapter and by debates on the ordination of homosexual persons in various denominations, concerns about homosexual civil rights ordinances, and the like.

In the *Christian Medical Society Journal,* Lewis Penhall Bird commented on the decision of the American Psychiatric Association to declassify homosexuality as a psychiatric disorder: "As with other controversial subjects, the issues used to be firmly settled. Now 'everything that was nailed down is comin' loose'." Bird went on to point out that Christians—including those in the conservative evangelical camp—have revised their views on at least three other sexual practices: sexual intercourse during menstruation, masturbation, and oral-genital sex. Although he did not attempt to resolve the problems surrounding the homosexuality issue, Bird did raise a number of questions to help Christian counselors think through this and other matters relating to human sexuality.[4]

To Bird's three sex-related issues on which Christians have recently been changing their minds, we could add a fourth—contraception. But that issue is too far afield and much too complex to consider here. Bird noted that at one time masturbation, oral-genital sex, and coitus during menstruation were considered *deviant* sexual practices ("defined as abnormal, unnatural, unhealthy, and/or sinful"). Now many Christian writers and counselors have reclassified them as *variant* sexual practices (sexual conduct "considered to be within normal limits," a variation).

The Bible is silent on the topics of masturbation and oral-genital sex, although the church has by no means been silent over the ages and has condemned both as sin in God's sight. It might be wise for us to focus on the third of the topics on which thinking has recently been revised, coitus during menstruation, because it would seem to be more parallel to the case of rethinking homosexuality. Both abusive homosexual practices and intercourse during menstruation are condemned in Scripture.

AN ILLUMINATING PARALLEL

Bird's only comment on this topic is that "few modern evangelicals would advocate excommunication (Leviticus 18:19–30) for couples who engage in intercourse during menstruation."

However, not only have there been few negative attacks; some Christian writers and counselors positively *encourage* the practice, and some do not so much as *hint* that any prohibition of the practice is found in the Bible.

Medical doctor Ed Wheat, for example, gives this advice: "A wife's sex drive ordinarily does not diminish during the menstrual period; so if both partners desire intercourse at this time, it's perfectly all right. If the wife has a diaphragm for birth control, she may insert it during the time of light bleeding and even have intercourse without any blood coming into the lower vagina."[5] And another counselor, Herbert Miles, even uses a variant on the natural law argument, claiming that if the Creator made woman in such a way that her peak sexual desire is right before, during, and after her menstrual period, "He must have meant for her need to be satisfied under the right circumstances."[6] However, if a homosexual person were to claim that God intended his or her sexual needs "to be satisfied under the right circumstances," that person would likely be accused of twisting Scripture. This is mentioned only to show that even in the most conservative Christian circles, a consistent system of interpreting Scripture is seldom applied. In spite of declarations of firm adherence to principle, there is far more accommodation to human experience in interpreting and applying Scripture than many Christians would care to admit.

Tim and Beverly LaHaye recognize the problem and address themselves to the biblical prohibition. Pointing out that intercourse during menstruation is not viewed as harmful by most medical authorities, they suggest that it should not be viewed as sinful because the death of Christ did away with all the ceremonial laws and rituals. Furthermore, they explain, "those laws were given thirty-five hundred years ago, before showers and baths were so convenient, before tampons, disinfectants, and other improved

means of sanitation had been invented."[7] The authors refer only
to the instructions about menstruation in Leviticus, chapter 15,
but do not quote from Leviticus, chapter 20. Verse 18 of chapter
20 says that "if a man lies with a woman during her monthly
period and brings shame upon her, he has exposed her discharge
and she has uncovered the source of her discharge; they shall both
be cut off from their people." Although the LaHayes neglect
Leviticus, chapter 20, concerning coitus during menstruation,
they latch on to it in their discussion of homosexuality. As we saw
earlier, they put great stress on verse 13: "If a man has intercourse
with a man as with a woman, they both commit an abomination.
They shall be put to death."

One could, of course, attempt to resolve the inconsistency in
treatment by arguing, as the LaHayes do, that in the one case the
command relates only to ceremonial law, while in the other it is
part of moral law. But such a distinction simply will not hold up
in the light of the twenty-second chapter of Ezekiel. Sins are
listed in Ezekiel, chapter 22, that call forth God's judgment,
including violations of sexual prohibitions that are also found in
Leviticus, chapter 20, and which seem to imply a moral violation
rather than merely a breaking of ceremonial taboos. Singled out
are incest, adultery, and intercourse during menstruation; homosexual acts, on the other hand, are not mentioned at all! Furthermore, a number of commentators think that all the sexual trans-
gressions on the list are equally serious to Ezekiel. Referring
specifically to the statement about intercourse during menstruation, Bible scholar H. L. Ellison writes: "What needs to be
stressed is that Ezekiel sees in offenses against the natural modes-
ties of sex (verse 10b) and in adultery (verse 11a) evils as great and
as deadly as incest and promiscuity of the worst sort."[8]

We certainly do not wish to argue that intercourse during
menstruation should be considered sinful for Christians. One

could point, for example, to Paul's instructions that married couples not abstain from sexual relations except for specific periods set aside for prayer by mutual consent (1 Cor. 7:5), or to Jesus' breaking of the taboos against touch with regard to the woman "who had had a flow of blood for twelve years" (Mark 5:25–34, RSV). We could also point to passages about changes in the ceremonial law, although no passage is *specifically* addressed to the regulations concerning menstruation. What is important to notice is simply that in view of medical opinion and personal experience, Christians have been willing to ignore commands about coitus during menstruation. Therefore, couldn't it be looked upon as a parallel case that some Christians are also rethinking the matter of homosexuality? As in the case of coitus during menstruation, the rethinking is partially due to medical opinion and other research, and partially due to the personal experience and needs of individuals. The parallel is worth pondering.

CANDIDATES FOR HELL, OR FOR GOD'S GRACE?

In the thinking, writing, and speaking of many Christians, probably no other group has been singled out as "candidates for hell" as consistently as homosexuals. Usually such condemnations are backed up with 1 Cor. 6:9–10, because the list of those who will not "possess the kingdom of God" includes those who participate in specific kinds of "homosexual perversion." As we commented in chapter 5, other categories are often overlooked, such as that of the covetous or greedy, who are never singled out by Christians for the kind of judgment categorically passed on homosexual persons. This select use of Scripture becomes even more clear when we turn to Gal. 5:19–21 which again describes those who "will never inherit the kingdom of God." Nothing about homosexuality is mentioned, but "quarrels, a contentious temper, envy, fits of rage, selfish ambitions, dissensions, party intrigues, and jealousies" *are* mentioned—and all of them are sins that seem to be very much at home in the average church! Persons who engage in them are seldom the subject of sermon topics setting forth God's judgment; it is much easier to make scapegoats of homosexuals. But Jesus warned us that judgment is a boomerang (Matt. 7:1); and the cumulative effect of scapegoating has been a legalistic and fearful withdrawal from the unlimited and unconditional love of God, and from the glorious liberty of the children of God.

For the sake of honesty in our interpretation and application of Scripture, as well as for the sake of justice and compassion, the time now seems ripe to take an altogether new approach to homosexuality. Some Christians are beginning to do this. Both independently and in mainline denominations, groups of homosexual Christians have been formed in recent years. Among them are Dignity (Roman Catholic), Integrity (Episcopalian), Gay Lutherans, and the Metropolitan Community Churches. In other cases, both heterosexual and homosexual Christians have come together for dialogue, understanding, and policy decisions. Such dialogue played an important role in a change of attitudes toward homosexual persons in the Netherlands. In the United States, a national task force, Evangelicals Concerned, was founded by psychotherapist Ralph Blair. The heterosexual and homosexual evangelicals who make up the group are "concerned about the lack of preparation for dealing realistically with homosexuality in the evangelical community and about the implications of the Gospel in the lives of gay men and women."[9]

THE CURRENT CHRISTIAN SPECTRUM, PART ONE:
HOMOSEXUALITY AS SIN

Even apart from such specialized groups, there seems to be developing among Christians of various persuasions a *continuum* or *spectrum* of views on the topic of homosexuality. On the one end are those who take the absolute position that homosexuality is sin. "The New Testament blasts homosexual activity as the lowest, most degraded kind of immorality," writes one person of this persuasion.[10] On the other end of the spectrum are those who would agree with Ralph Blair that it is time for Christians "to abandon un-Biblical crusades against homosexuality and to help those who have quite naturally developed along homosexual lines to accept themselves as Jesus Christ has accepted them—just as they are—and to live lives which include responsible homosexual behavior."[11] (A similar view is held by Troy Perry and the Metropolitan Community Church).[12] In between those two ends of the spectrum there are a variety of views, some of which include a great deal of compassionate and concerned questioning.

Even those who stand firmly on the "sin perspective" end of the continuum are increasingly careful to draw a distinction between the homosexual *condition* (orientation) and homosexual *activities*. According to this perspective, *being* a homosexual isn't sinful, but *practicing* homosexuality is. In a position paper put out by the Presbyterians United for Biblical Concerns (a conservative group within the United Presbyterian Church U.S.A.), it was stated that the ordination of avowed, practicing homosexuals would be "a grievous offense against God," but that a "repentant, non-practicing homosexual may be considered for ordination."[13] Group representatives explain that theological evaluation of current literature has not convinced them "that the church should change its position and approve of homosexual practice" after uniformly opposing it throughout church history.

According to Presbyterians United for Biblical Concerns, "male and female homosexuality is a condition of disordered sexuality which may be attributed to the fall of humankind, and reflects the brokenness of our sinful world." This group feels that the answer for the homosexual person lies in repentance, healing, and change. A similar stance was taken by the 1975 Continental Congress on the Family, a nationwide interdenominational gathering of over two thousand evangelicals. The official statement opposed the "unjust and unkind treatment given to homosexuals by individuals, society, and the Church" and called for ministry "to those who are homosexually oriented in order to help them to change their life-style in a manner which brings glory to God." While indicating that "the Bible teaches homosexuality to be sinful," the Congress acknowledged "that a homosexual orientation can be the result of having been sinned against." Thus the call is for understanding, forgiveness, and spiritual support on the part of Christians who care about helping homosexuals.[14]

THE CURRENT CHRISTIAN SPECTRUM, PART TWO: CONCERN
FOR PERSONS AND RELATIONSHIPS

For some Christians, there seems to be a new focus on the individual, rather than on homosexuality in the abstract. Evangelical author Joseph Bayly makes this candid confession: "For years I have been troubled by a strict application of the Bible's strong condemnation of homosexuality, and total judgment of the homosexual person. . . . I accept the Bible's authority; at the same time I have wondered—as with suicide—about a precise identification of every person of this type with the biblical model."[15]

Other Christians, besides moving beyond the matter of homosexual acts to consider the homosexual person, have been taking a fresh look at homosexual *relationships*. "Perhaps we have been asking the wrong questions about such relationships," suggests Margaret Evening. "The emphasis seems to have been merely on whether or not homosexual acts are morally permissible . . . when the primary consideration should be: 'Is this friendship going to radiate love *out* to others and draw them *in* to its circle . . . ?' " She introduces a number of considerations about how a loving relationship can be a "center of healing and comfort, open and available to all amid the wounds and sores of society."[16]

THE CURRENT CHRISTIAN SPECTRUM, PART THREE:
ACCEPTANCE OF HOMOSEXUAL UNION

A minority of Christians—apparently a growing minority—suggest that a compassionate and creative solution to the homosexual problem lies in the acceptance of committed, permanent homosexual unions. The Jesuit priest John McNeill is one who holds this view. He backs it up with theological, biblical, and practical arguments in his 1976 book, *The Church and the Homosexual.* But he is not alone.

As the members of the United Methodist Church continue to discuss the decision of the General Conference to prohibit avowed homosexuals from entering the United Methodist ministry, some thoughtful dissenting opinions are being presented. For instance, after attending the Good News Convocation in Anderson, Indiana, where full support was given to the General Conference decision, Mary F. Clark, a professional mental health worker, wrote a paper describing her "feelings of unrest" about the principles used in "drawing lines." She questions the distinction between *being* a homosexual and being a *practicing* homosexual, since "being inactive sexually does not make anyone less homosexual or heterosexual." She also questions the practice of allowing homosexuals to be part of a congregation while barring them from the ministry, since "not making the highest post in the church available to anyone puts them in a second-rate position at best." She asks why, since greed is mentioned along with homosexual abuses in 1 Cor. 6:9, the church has not passed a motion to bar greedy people from the clergy. She also wonders why the church has not to date held any dialogue with homosexuals; and she wonders "What should the gay United Methodist ministers and lay people do at this point (as in fact the church already has both)." She suggests that the church "show integrity" by "presenting and studying all sides equally," and concludes by saying that it is "better to admit an error than to walk in it."[17]

An associate professor of Theology at Drew University, Darrell J. Doughty, presented a paper to a local meeting of United Presbyterians which was then made available to the denomination in *Church and Society* magazine. Drawing an analogy between the homosexual issue and the first-century issue concerning whether all non-Jewish converts to Christianity should have to be circumcised, an issue which "stirred up passions of ferocious intensity," Professor Doughty points out that the first-century problem was solved by the triumph of grace over the law. Similarly, although the rabbis taught that "a man without a woman is not a man," neither Jesus nor Paul was married; and when Paul discussed marriage in 1 Corinthians, chapter 7, he made no appeal to nature or to creation or to the necessity of procreation, but only to the relationship between the persons directly involved. Defining sin as "the manipulation and exploitation of other persons in the attempt to establish and elevate ourselves," Doughty argues that "if we condemn homosexuality as contrary to the Will of God, and refuse ordination and perhaps even church membership to homosexual persons, then the burden is on us to show that homosexual relationships cannot be relationships of love. . . . and that our decision is not simply an attempt to justify ourselves."[18]

At the 1975 annual meetings of the Christian Association for Psychological Studies, a symposium on homosexuality brought together a panel of Christians in the mental health professions. They explained that behavioral science research and the realities of their clinical practice had forced them to take a new look at the traditional biblical interpretations which distinguish between a homosexual orientation and homosexual behavior, but which see all such behavior as sinful. They suggested an alternative view: namely, that promiscuity, fornication, and adultery should be regarded as sinful for both homosexual and heterosexual persons, but that a loving, committed, permanent relationship between two persons of the same sex was in an entirely different category and was not condemned in Scripture. According to a *Christianity Today* news report, the majority view expressed by members of the panel was that "God's 'perfect' will is for the monogamous heterosexual family. However . . . Christians burdened with an involuntary homosexual orientation could choose a committed homosexual relationship as within God's 'permissive' will rather than an unwanted celibacy."[19] Gay activists and many other homosexuals might not appreciate the implication of second-class Christianity in that statement. But since the acceptance of life-long homosexual unions would solve a great many problems and provide helpful guidelines for both ethical living and ordination decisions, this alternative to traditional attitudes is worth exploring in greater depth.

❀ 9. Proposing a Homosexual Christian Ethic

To ACCEPT the position taken by the panel majority at the Christian Association for Psychological Studies would require a major shift in thinking for many Christians—a shift from one "model" to another, while maintaining a concern for theological implications and a desire to know and follow God's plan for human sexuality. On the opposite page are the two models in graphic form.

For most Christians, such a shift in thinking will not come easily. It is, after all, a different way of looking at the topic, and it goes against the traditional teachings. Some Christian leaders, sensitive to the problems on both sides of the issue, seem to reach the alternative view rather grudgingly or adopt some position in between the two views. Lewis Smedes, an evangelical theologian and ethics professor, provides an example of what we might call "cautious accommodation."

CAUTIOUS ACCOMMODATION

Smedes suggests that a homosexual Christian should seek a change in sexual orientation if at all possible. But if change is impossible and "constitutional homosexuality" is real, says

MODEL I—The Traditional View

God's Ideal for the Sexual Expression of Love	Abuses
Heterosexual, monogamous marriage	Fornication
	Adultery
	Promiscuity
	Homosexuality

MODEL II—The Alternative View

God's Ideal for the Sexual Expression of Love	Abuses of God's Plan for Human Sexuality for both Heterosexual and Homosexual Persons
A covenantal heterosexual relationship (marriage)	Fornication (sex apart from having entered the permanent, committed, covenant relationship)
A covenantal homosexual relationship (for persons of homosexual orientation)	Adultery (unfaithfulness to the person to whom one is committed, or causing another person to be unfaithful to the one to whom he or she is pledged)
	Promiscuity (sex with a variety of partners, casual sex based on lust, exploitation of others, etc.)

Smedes, then two other options exist: celibacy or "optimum homosexual morality." According to Smedes, celibacy is to be preferred—even though he admits that such a course is likely to be difficult. The emphasis is not on converting to heterosexuality but on abstaining from homosexual practices. "Ordinarily no one has the right to prescribe celibacy for another person," writes Smedes. "But in view of the judgment that homosexual life is ethically unwarranted and personally unsatisfying, the choice should be seriously weighed."

Being a realist, however, Smedes points out that neither change nor celibacy may work out for some homosexual persons.

What then? He suggests that there should be developed the "best ethical conditions" for living out one's sexual life. Specifically, that would mean "no exploitation, no seduction, and no enticement of youth into the homosexual sphere." It would also mean intense development of the nonsexual aspects of life, and efforts toward building stable relationships, "associations in which respect and regard for the other as a person dominates their sexual relationship." But Smedes emphasizes strongly that, in his view, "to develop a morality for the homosexual life is *not* to accept homosexual practices as morally commendable. It is, however, to recognize that the optimum moral life within a deplorable situation is preferable to a life of sexual chaos."[1]

Counselors who think of homosexuality in more positive terms also are careful to suggest that the person who feels he or she is developing in a homosexual direction should be absolutely *sure* of a homosexual orientation before embarking on a course based on such an assumption. Societal attitudes can make the lot of the homosexual a difficult one. It is especially hard to sustain a long-term, faithful sexual union when social pressures are all in the direction of divisiveness. Whereas pressures on heterosexual married couples offer great incentives and rewards for staying together, homosexual unions are beset with pressures to split them apart. Because of these and similar practical handicaps, it is a kindness to advise persons whose drive could be channeled in a heterosexual direction to go in that direction if at all possible. (On the other hand, it is *not* a kindness to push young persons into heterosexual marriage if they still have some doubts about their orientation). The Anglican theologian Norman Pittenger, one of the few writers who has attempted to develop "an ethic for homosexuals," has a brief but pertinent discussion of such considerations in his book *Time for Consent: A Christian's Approach to Homosexuality.*[2]

Helmut Thielicke, a renowned evangelical theologian in Germany, provides a thought-provoking and well-informed discussion of homosexuality in his book, *The Ethics of Sex*. Having studied the relevant medical and psychological research, Thielicke is appalled at the inaccurate and uninformed statements about homosexuality in the literature of Protestant theology. He recognizes that "constitutional homosexuality . . . is largely unsusceptible to medical or psychotherapeutic treatment, at least so far as achieving the desired goal of a fundamental conversion to normality is concerned." He argues that when an "ailment" is "recognized as incurable," our attitude toward it must change; we must "accept" it. He defines acceptance rather courageously: "to accept the burden of the predisposition to homosexuality only as a divine dispensation and see it as a task to be wrestled with, indeed— paradoxical as it may sound—to think of it as a talent to be invested (Luke 19:13 ff.)."

Thielicke establishes that constitutional homosexuality is an ethical issue and definitely not a matter for criminal prosecution, except when involving acts with minors, indecent public display, or prostitution. And he explains that "the homosexual has to realize his optimal ethical potentialities *on the basis* of his irreversible situation. . . . It is the question of how the homosexual in his actual situation can achieve the optimal ethical potential of sexual self-realization."

Thielicke rejects the widespread solution of requiring celibacy of all homosexuals who want to live Christianly, pointing out that "celibacy is based upon a special calling and, moreover, is an act of free will." He does not want to require of the homosexual "a degree of harshness and rigor which one would never think of demanding of a 'normal' person." In light of the various special problems faced by the homosexual who wants to live biblically, Thielicke recommends that Christians exhibit a great deal of pastoral care which does *not* expose the homosexual to "defamation of his urge."

Thielicke sees "an acceptable partnership" such as we have proposed as an ideal solution, and cites evidence concerning the achievement of "stable, 'monogamous' relationships among homosexuals." However, because he thinks that the enormous pressures brought to bear against homosexuals make the achievement of such a union a truly exceptional one, he assumes that "Christian pastoral care will have to be concerned primarily with helping the person to *sublimate* his homosexual urge."

Foremost among the pressures endured by homosexual Christians, according to Thielicke, is the fact that "the homosexual does not have the benefit of living within a supportive order that is informed by a traditional ethos such as that of the institution of marriage. Instead of having at his disposal at set of prefabricated decisions which are made for him by the tradition and make it easier for him to find his way about, he is to an unimaginably greater degree thrown back upon himself."[3]

ETHICAL STANCES IN THE NETHERLANDS

Another author who calls for "a viable homosexual ethic" is J. Rinzema, pastor of a Reformed Church in the Netherlands. He urges Christian moralists to "develop a morality for homosexuality in consultation with homosexual people." Such a morality would encourage permanent relationships for constitutional (unchangeable) homosexuals, and would include the provision of guidelines for such matters as courtship and decisions to form a permanent union, and then for living within that union. "As there are rules for the relationships between married people," writes Rinzema, "we believe that society must both create room for and find rules by which homosexual people can live together in permanent relationships."[4]

Rinzema knows what he's talking about in suggesting that heterosexual Christian leaders get together with homosexual persons for discussion, because that is exactly what has been done in the Netherlands. Holland is one of the few places in the Western world where there is relatively little discrimination against homosexuals. Educational efforts, changes in laws, scientific research, and changing attitudes within the churches have all had an impact on public awareness of homosexuals as fellow human beings with much to contribute to society. In the early 1960s, a working group of Roman Catholics and Protestants was formed for discussion of the issue. Through this organization (Pastoral Help for Homophiles), heterosexual and homosexual Christians could share their perspectives in an effort to develop a sensitivity to and an understanding of one another.

Similarly, the churches of the Netherlands made an effort to rethink Scripture and theology with regard to homosexuality, and some efforts were made toward the formation of ethical principles as well. For example, a Roman Catholic priest issued a set of guidelines which, among other suggestions, encouraged ministers to help homosexuals build up stable relationships and to realize that sexual abstinence "is not to be seen as a natural thing for the homosexual and is in fact exceptional." Pastors were instructed to help homosexual persons see the importance of faithfulness within a relationship. Near the top of the list were two especially crucial guidelines: (1) "a stable relationship must never be broken," and (2) heterosexual marriage must be rejected as a solution for homosexuality.[5]

The last two guidelines mentioned need to be heard by those Christians who have caused excruciating mental and emotional torture by trying to break up a relationship between two persons who deeply love each other. Any counselor who gets involved with the real hurts of human beings is likely to have run into some cases of this sort. Likewise, the problems of homosexual persons who have entered heterosexual marriages in the hope that this will bring about a "cure" or change of orientation are also familiar to counselors. The tragedy here is not only the homosexual person's pain, but also the anguish suffered by the spouse—which is intensified all the more if children have been born of the union. Unfaithfulness and eventual marital breakup are not at all uncommon in such situations. Better they had never been entered into in the first place.

Some Christians in the Netherlands, like some Christians the world over, remain unconvinced that homosexual acts can *ever* be right—even in a stable, committed relationship. Certain Dutch Christians have argued that "if some women who cannot find husbands can abstain from sexual contact, so can the homosexual."[6] A similar position is taken in an InterVarsity publication, *The Returns of Love,* which candidly describes the struggles of a young Christian fighting to resist his homosexual impulses and live a celibate life.[7]

CELIBACY: A SPECIAL GIFT, OR A CONDITION FOR SALVATION?

But if these Christians find it impossible to reconcile the idea of homosexual expression with Christian theology, others find it difficult to reconcile required homosexual celibacy with Christian theology. We have already mentioned the view of Helmut Thielicke that celibacy is a "special calling" and "an act of free will." Similarly, theology professor Daniel C. Maguire takes issue with the Vatican's 1976 "Declaration on Certain Questions Concerning Sexual Ethics." Maguire argues that in Catholic theology, celibacy is seen as "a precious gift" given by God only to certain persons. "Yet when we move with the Declaration to homosexual persons," says Maguire, "the precious gift is normative and a necessary condition for salvation. . . . For the heterosexual person the Declaration recalls St. Paul's practical advice that it is better to marry than to burn." Yet for homosexual persons as a group, "there is no alternative to burning . . . unless, of course, they are all charismatically gifted" with the "precious gift" of celibacy.[8] Thus, Maguire points out that the Vatican is more strict concerning homosexuals than heterosexuals.

THE CREATION ACCOUNTS: HETEROSEXUALITY, OR COHUMANITY?

For many Christians, the biggest barrier to accepting the possibility of homosexual unions pertains to an understanding of the creation accounts in chapters 1, 2, and 5 of Genesis and in Jesus' commentary on them in Matthew, chapter 19. David Fraser, for example, relates the creation account to the Song of Solomon and argues thus: "That God's image is both male and female, not simply being-in-community, has ramifications beyond Genesis one. The Song presumes erotic love to be heterosexual and the rest of revelation reinforces that conviction."[9] But theologian Theodore Jennings takes a different perspective, suggesting that our being created male and female in the image of God is a way of understanding that "the crucial determinant of our humanity" is *cohumanity.* "That our humanity is cohumanity cannot be interpreted only in a sexual or genital way," says Jennings. "If this is done, nothing remains of the symbolic and thus ethical significance of cohumanity. We have then literalized the metaphor so as to deprive it of its general ethical significance."[10]

Rosemary Radford Ruether, a professor of historical theology, applies the concept of cohumanity specifically to homosexual unions:

Once sex is no longer confined to procreative genital acts and masculinity and femininity are exposed as social ideologies, then it is no longer possible to argue that sex/love between two persons of the same sex cannot be a valid embrace of bodily selves expressing love. If sex/love is centered primarily on communion between two persons rather than on biological concepts of procreative complementarity, then the love of two persons of the same sex need be no less than that of two persons of the opposite sex. Nor need their experience of ecstatic bodily communion be less valuable.[11]

It seems to us that the Genesis creation accounts imply that male and female are meant to relate to one another *as* male and female, both of them made in the image of God and both of them responsible for the stewardship of the created world. But if we take the creation accounts to mean that relating as male and female can only mean genital relating in heterosexual marriage, we have excluded all persons who are single (for whatever reason —illness, handicaps, preference, and so forth) from any place in the cooperative union of cohumanity.

It should be obvious that male-female relating in society goes far beyond genital relating. It is perhaps less obvious, but nevertheless true according to homosexuals themselves, that homosexual persons continue to think of themselves as either male or female and continue to enjoy non-genital friendships with the other sex. In other words, heterosexual men and women can relate authentically as male and female in a social group without having genital relations with everybody of the other sex. And single persons can participate in social activities with the other sex, affirming cohumanity, without having genital relations with any representative of the other sex. Similarly, homosexual Christians can enter a same-sex union without breaking the cohumanity of creation, because they can continue to relate to the other sex as male and female in non-genital ways.

ARE WE PERPETUATING THE FALLEN ORDER?

Another issue brought up by certain Christians is this: if heterosexual monogamy is the *ideal* according to God's design for human sexuality—even if the possibility of stable homosexual relationships could be said to lie within the "permissive" will of God for persons incapable of heterosexual relationships—aren't we failing homosexual persons if we don't help them strive for the "ideal"? If homosexuality exists because of the fall described in Genesis, chapter 3, (since only two heterosexual persons were in the world before that), these Christians ask, then aren't we perpetuating the "fallen order" by not steering homosexual persons toward a change of orientation and heterosexual marriage? And if we say that such change is not possible, aren't we denying the redemptive power of Jesus Christ to "save to the uttermost" and make all things new?

The issue is a complex one. Some would reply to the above questions that it is necessary to proceed from an understanding of psychological research, including an awareness of how deep-rooted sexual self-identity is, and then go on to speak of God's meeting individuals *where they are* and bringing good out of what appears to be "less than the ideal." Others would say that if certain persons are equally heterosexual and homosexual, or if their homosexual urge is weaker than the heterosexual one, they should certainly be encouraged to structure their lives in accordance with social norms and "God's ideal." (Of course it must be recognized that this view does nothing for those who are predominantly or exclusively homosexual.) Still other Christians would take issue with the notion that heterosexuality is God's ideal in the first place—at least if the idea carries with it the implication that homosexual persons are somehow "second best." Thus, Father John McNeill asks, "How can Christian homosexuals accept themselves and their homosexuality with any sense of their own dignity and value as long as they must see themselves and their actions as organically expressing the effects of sin in the world . . . ?" In McNeill's view, "the homosexual is here according to God's will," and "God has a divine purpose in so creating human nature that a certain percentage of human beings are homosexual."[12]

James Nelson, Professor of Christian Ethics at United Theological Seminary of the Twin Cities, would agree. He argues that "same-sex relationships are fully capable of expressing God's humanizing intentions," and views the "homosexual problem" as "more truly a heterosexual problem" (of homophobia), just as the "woman problem" is a problem of "male sexism." He commends the 1973 statement of the Executive Council of the United Church of Christ concerning the full acceptance of homosexual persons symbolized by ordination: "In the instance of considering a stated homosexual's candidacy for ordination the issue should not be his/her homosexuality as such, but rather the candidate's total view of human sexuality and his/her understanding of the morality of its use."[13]

THE HIGH PRICE OF CARING

At this point, it should be crystal clear that the questions surrounding homosexuality in Christian perspective are far from settled. There is no uniform opinion among Christians and in fact a great deal of disagreement. But as more and more persons become less afraid of the topic and more sensitive to the issues involved, a solid groundwork is being laid for creative rethinking on the theological/biblical/ethical level and for compassionate counsel on the practical/personal level.

Those who dare to pioneer in such rethinking must be prepared to pay a price. Deeply ingrained attitudes toward taboo subjects do not disappear overnight. Even to suggest a reexamination of the subject can call forth charges that a person is guilty of heresy, of leaving Chrsitian teachings and going against the will of God. For instance, when the ecumenical radio minister for the Netherlands prayed for homosexuals during one of his broadcasts in 1959, he received an avalanche of mail, not only from grateful homosexuals and "confused homosexuals who could not believe that he as a minister could do such a thing," but also from confused and angry colleagues and persons who accused him of blasphemy and ignorance of the Bible. Yet his courage in bringing the topic out in the open helped pave the way for the change of attitude that took place in his country.[14]

In spite of known discrimination against homosexuals, law professor Walter Barnett asserts, "it has not yet become fashionable to champion the cause of this minority group." A civil rights enthusiast could stand up for the cause of a racial minority, Barnett explains, without worrying that others might raise questions about his or her own skin color (not that it should matter!). Skin color won't rub off on someone else, but "the aura of 'immorality' can."[15] The implications of this for concerned Christians come through in a statement from Erving Goffman's classic work on stigma: "In general, the tendency for a stigma to spead from the stigmatized to his close connections provides a reason why such relations tend either to be avoided or to be terminated where existing."[16]

John McNeill, alert to the same problem, writes that an effective counseling ministry to homosexual persons can ruin a minister's career and destroy his reputation. He quotes a report of The National Federation of Priests' Councils which notes that "individual priests and ministers, working with homosexuals, usually encounter a social and psychological stigma as a result of their work, and this stigma is the single most effective obstacle to ministers who want to work with homosexuals."[17]

THE BIG QUESTION FOR US ALL

The big question is this: Are we willing to face the cost in order to share the love of Jesus Christ? In chapter 2 we noted how, in Mark Twain's novel *The Adventures of Huckleberry Finn*, Huck wrestles through a moral dilemma about demonstrating true friendship to a stigmatized person of his day—a man who wore the dual stigma of blackness in a racist society and slavery in an exploitative one. To help his friend Jim escape meant violating not only human law but also divine law as it had been interpreted in that society, because to help a slave escape meant stealing property from its owner. Not only did Huck worry about God and about going to hell for obeying the impulse of his heart, but he also worried about what people would think of him. "It would get all around that Huck Finn helped a nigger to get his freedom; and if I was ever to see anybody from that town again I'd be ready to get down and lick his boots for shame."[18] But such worries did not prevent him from doing what he felt to be right.

Jesus knew all about stigma. He never hesitated to move among the oppressed persons of his day, including the most despised social outcasts. He went about his ministry without worrying about the aspersions cast upon his character, his motives, his righteousness. "If this fellow were a real prophet," said some, "He would know who this woman is that touches him, and what sort of woman she is, a sinner" (Luke 7:39). He ignored the insinuations and seemed unconcerned about reputation. "Look at him!" said others, "a glutton and a drinker, a friend of tax-gatherers and sinners!" (Luke 7:34).

Jesus was not afraid of being called names, nor was he afraid to be identified with the most hated, discredited persons in the society in which he lived. He cared about them. He felt their pain, knew their hunger and thirst, recognized their humanity, saw the image of God in them. In short, he loved them. And he longed to minister to them—even if others misunderstood and criticized. Name-calling was as common then as it is now, and to label someone with a scornful term identified with a stigmatized group has always been considered an extreme insult. Today, the terms of insult are frequently associated with homosexuality—"queer," "dyke," "flit," "butch," "faggot." When Jesus walked the earth, the stigmatized persons were the Samaritans; and the term of insult was "You *Samaritan!*"

Jesus was willing to be called a Samaritan (John 8:48). He made no effort at denial. He refused to dissociate himself from this disdained group, and as we saw in chapter 3, he chose the example of a Samaritan to illustrate the principle of neighbor-love. Are we willing to follow Christ's example? Even when fulfilling the second great commandment may seem to go against tradition and public opinion?

The Reverend Paul Oestreicher, an Anglican priest and the Chairman of Amnesty International, remarked on the British Broadcasting Corporation that "the hero of . . . [Christ's] best-known parable was a Samaritan, the Jew's most hated enemy. 'Go and be like him,' said Jesus . . . like that atheist, that communist, that fascist, that homosexual . . . like whomever we most love to hate."[19]

"Love your neighbor as yourself," we are told (Matt. 22:39). "No one has greater love than the one who lays down his life for his friends," we are told (John 15:13, NIV).

Who is my neighbor?
Who is my friend?
Could it be the Samaritan?
Could it be the homosexual?

Notes

1. WHO IS MY NEIGHBOR?

1. As quoted by John Lauritsen, *Religious Roots of the Taboo on Homosexuality* (New York: privately printed, 1974), pp. 23–24.
2. Anita Bryant, as quoted in Bob Reiss, "New Battleground: Gay Rights Begins to Make an Impact," *Us*, June 14, 1977, p. 75.
3. Anita Bryant, as quoted in "Battle Over Gay Rights," *Newsweek*, June 6, 1977, p. 22.
4. Unidentified minister, quoted in Ibid., p. 16.
5. Jerry Falwell, quoted in Ibid., p. 22.
6. Quoted in Reiss, p. 75.
7. "Playboy Interview: Jimmy Carter," *Playboy* 23 (November, 1976), p. 69. See also our chapter 4.
8. Quoted in "Platform," *National Courier* 2 (April 15, 1977), p. 21.
9. Sigmund Freud, "The Psychogenesis of a Case of Homosexuality in a Woman," *Collected Papers*, vol. 2 (New York: Basic Books, 1959), pp. 206–7.
10. "Torture, Homosexuality, and the Cry for Hope," *The Other Side* 13 (April, 1977), p. 6.
11. Ruth Simpson, *From the Closet to the Courts* (New York: Penguin Books, 1977), pp. 146–47.

2. THE RISKS AND CHALLENGES OF MORAL GROWTH

1. *Huck Finn and His Critics*, ed. Richard Lettis, et. al. (New York: Macmillan, 1962), p. 187.
2. *Huck Finn*, pp. 188–89.
3. See Letha Scanzoni and Nancy Hardesty, *All We're Meant To Be* (Waco: Word, 1974); Paul K. Jewett, *Man as Male and Female* (Grand Rapids, Mich.: Eerdmans, 1975); and Virginia R. Mollenkott, *Women, Men, and the Bible* (Nashville: Abingdon, 1977).
4. G. C. Berkouwer, *Holy Scripture* (Grand Rapids, Mich.: Eerdmans, 1975), p. 137.

5. Berkouwer, p. 137.
6. As cited by Berkouwer, p. 138.
7. John Milton, *Samson Agonistes*, line 41. For a discussion of Milton's brilliant dramatization of Samson's final hours, see Virginia R. Mollenkott, "Relativism in *Samson Agonistes*," *Studies in Philology* 67 (January, 1970): 89–102.
8. John Calvin, *Institutes of the Christian Religion*, trans. Henry Beveridge, 2 vols. (Grand Rapids, Mich.: Eerdmans, 1975), 2:137.

3. THE HOMOSEXUAL AS SAMARITAN

1. "Can the Risk Be Cut?" *Newsweek*, October 6, 1975, p. 20; " 'Gays' and the Press," *Newsweek*, October 20, 1975, pp. 93–94.
2. Pierre Berton, *The Comfortable Pew* (Philadelphia: Lippincott, 1965), p. 78.
3. Personal interview. For a full report, see Letha Scanzoni, "Conservative Christians and Gay Civil Rights," *Christian Century* 93 (October 13, 1976): 857–62; and "Gay Confrontation," *Christianity Today* 20 (March 12, 1976): 633–35.
4. "God Is Just a Prayer Away," radio broadcast originating in Lynchburg, Ohio. The sermon described was presented on the October 31, 1976 program.
5. Tim and Beverly LaHaye, *The Act of Marriage* (Grand Rapids, Mich.: Zondervan, 1976), p. 261.
6. John Lauritsen and David Thorstad, *The Early Homosexual Rights Movement (1864–1935)* (New York: Times Change Press, 1974), p. 44.
7. All of these persons are described in A. L. Rowse, *Homosexuals in History* (New York: Macmillan, 1977).
8. Except for Miss Woolley, all of these persons are described in Barbara Grier and Coletta Reid, *Lesbian Lives* (Baltimore: Diana Press, 1976). See also Jane Rule, *Lesbian Images* (New York: Pocket Books, 1976). On Miss Woolley, see Molly Ivins, "Book Calling Ex-Holyoke Head a Lesbian Is Assailed," *New York Times*, August 21, 1976.
9. William Shakespeare, Sonnet 20.
10. John T. Shawcross, "Milton and Diodati: An Essay in Psychodynamic Meaning," *Milton Studies* 7 (1975): 127–63.
11. Margaret Evening, *Who Walk Alone* (Downers Grove, Ill.: InterVarsity Press, 1974), pp. 63–64. This passage was greatly altered in the second printing. The publisher explained to us in personal correspondence that he had received many complaints about the section on homosexuality.
12. W. H. Auden, *Collected Longer Poems* (New York: Random House, 1969), pp. 181, 183–84. Reprinted by permission of Random House, Inc.
13. Matthew R. Brown, "Gerard Manley Hopkins: Exploding for Christ," *Christianity Today* 21 (January 7, 1977): 388–90.
14. Wendell Stacey Johnson, "Sexuality and Inscape," *The Hopkins Quarterly* 3 (July, 1976): 59–66. According to *Quarterly* editor Richard F. Giles, an article by Michael Lynch of the University of Toronto, forthcoming in *The Hopkins Quarterly*, will discuss Hopkins's homosexual orientation even more forcefully. See also the review

of E. E. Phare's book on Hopkins in *Criterion* 13 (April, 1934): 497–500, in which W. H. Auden flatly asserted that Hopkins's feelings were homosexual. And see the delicately worded discussion of Hopkins's homosexual condition in Peter Milward, S.J., and Raymond Schoder, S.J., *Landscape and Inscape: Vision and Inspiration in Hopkins' Poetry* (Grand Rapids, Mich.: Eerdmans, 1975), pp. 91–92.

15. *The Norton Anthology of English Literature* (New York: Norton, 1974), 2: 1742.
16. "The Lesbian Priest," *Time*, January 24, 1977, p. 58.
17. Elizabeth Moberly, "Homosexuality and the Church," *Christian* 4 (Annunciation 1977): 151.
18. Ibid.
19. Ibid.
20. *New York City Presbytery News* (May, 1977), pp. 2, 4.
21. Ibid., p. 4.
22. Ibid., p. 4.
23. Sylvia Rudolph, "One of Our Family Is Gay," *The Christian Home* 9 (May, 1977): 17. Concerning the revoking of Huskey's deacon's orders, returning him to lay status, see "Gay Deacon Loses Orders," *The Christian Century* 94 (August 17–24, 1977): 712–13.
24. Malcolm Boyd, *Am I Running With You, God?* (New York: Doubleday, 1977), p. 23. Reprinted by permission of Doubleday & Company, Inc.

4. STIGMA AND STEREOTYPING

1. "*Playboy* Interview: Jimmy Carter," *Playboy* 23 (November, 1976), p. 69.
2. Paul Rock, *Deviant Behavior* (London: Hutchinson & Co., 1973), p. 28.
3. Peter Berger and Thomas Luckman, *The Social Construction of Reality* (London: The Penguin Press, 1967), p. 48, as quoted in Rock, p. 29.
4. Personal interview. See Letha Scanzoni, "Conservative Christians and Gay Civil Rights," *Christian Century* 93 (October 13, 1976): 858.
5. Rock, p. 29.
6. E. Rubington and M. S. Weinberg, eds., *Deviance* (New York: Macmillan, 1968), p. 10, as quoted in Rock, p. 29.
7. Isobel Miller, *Patience and Sarah* (New York: McGraw-Hill, 1969). Originally published under the title *A Place for Us.*
8. Laura Z. Hobson, *Consenting Adult* (New York: Doubleday, 1975).
9. Howard Brown, M.D., *Familiar Faces, Hidden Lives* (New York: Harcourt Brace Jovanovich, 1976).
10. An article in the *New York Times* (March 9, 1976) pointed out that only recently have there been less embarrassment and more public acceptance of the fact of Whitman's homosexuality. In the past, writes John O'Connor, "that fact bubbled up into public controversy whenever a proposal was presented to name a bridge, a school, or an auditorium in honor of the poet. . . . more often than not, the proposal would be shelved."
11. Alex Davidson, *The Returns of Love* (London: InterVarsity Press, 1970), p. 18.

12. Rock, pp. 30–35.
13. N. K. Denzin, "Rules of Conduct and the Study of Deviant Behavior," in *Deviance and Respectability,* ed. J. Douglas (New York: Basic Books, 1970), p. 121, as quoted in Rock, p. 31.
14. Armand Nicholi II, "Homosexualism and Homosexuality," *Baker's Dictionary of Christian Ethics,* ed. Carl F. H. Henry (Grand Rapids, Mich.: Baker Book House, 1973), p. 296.
15. Erving Goffman, *Stigma* (Englewood Cliffs, N.J.: Prentice-Hall, 1963), p. 28.
16. The theory of cognitive dissonance was first set forth by Leon Festinger in his book, *A Theory of Cognitive Dissonance* (Stanford, Calif.: Stanford University Press, 1957).
17. Ascanio Condivi, "Michelangelo Buonarroti," in *The Portable Renaissance Reader,* ed. James Bruce Ross and Mary Martin McLaughlin (New York: Viking Press, 1953), p. 509.
18. Howard Brown, M.D., *Familiar Faces, Hidden Lives* (New York: Harcourt Brace Jovanovich, 1976), p. 32.
19. W. H. Auden, *The Dyer's Hand and Other Essays* (New York: Random House, 1962). See especially pp. 27, 71, 131–32, 158.
20. From *The Age of Anxiety* in *W. H. Auden: Collected Poems,* ed. Edward Mendelson (New York: Random House, 1976), p. 408. Used by permission of Random House, Inc.

5. WHAT DOES THE BIBLE SAY?

1. D. Sherwin Bailey, *Homosexuality and the Western Christian Tradition* (New York: Longmans, Green & Co., 1955), pp. 1–28.
2. "Homosexuality," in *Towards a Quaker View of Sex,* rev. ed. (London: Friends Home Service Committee, 1964), p. 33.
3. Walter Barnett, *Sexual Freedom and the Constitution* (Albuquerque: University of New Mexico Press, 1973), pp. 7, 23–39.
4. Susan Brownmiller, *Against Our Will: Men, Women, and Rape* (New York: Simon & Schuster, 1975).
5. Alan J. Davis, "Sexual Assaults in the Philadelphia Prison System and Sheriff's Vans," *Transaction* 6, No. 2 (1968), as reprinted in Chad Gordon and Gayle Johnson, eds., *Readings in Human Sexuality: Contemporary Perspectives* (New York: Harper & Row, 1976), pp. 155–56.
6. John L. McKenzie, *The World of the Judges* (Englewood Cliffs, N.J.: Prentice-Hall, 1966), p. 165.
7. John J. McNeill, *The Church and the Homosexual* (Kansas City: Sheed, Andrews & McMeel, 1976), p. 50.
8. McNeill, pp. 68–74.
9. Shabbath 65a and Yebamoth 76a. The Babylonian Talmud, 34 volumes, translated into English with notes, glossary, and indices under the editorship of I. Epstein (London: Soncino Press, 1935–1948), 7:311, 16:513.

10. Norman Pittenger, "The Homosexual Expression of Love," in *Is Gay Good?*, ed. W. Dwight Oberholtzer (Philadelphia: Westminster Press, 1971), p. 237.
11. McNeill, p. 169.
12. Morton Scott Enslin, *The Ethics of Paul* (Nashville: Abingdon Press, 1957), p. 9.
13. Margaret Evening, *Who Walk Alone* (Downers Grove, Ill.: InterVarsity Press, 1974), p. 57.
14. Enslin, p. 146.
15. Jack Wyrtzen, as quoted in "Battle Over Gay Rights," *Newsweek*, June 6, 1977, p. 22.
16. Alfred Kinsey et al., *Sexual Behavior in the Human Female* (Philadelphia: W. B. Saunders Co., 1953; repr. in Pocket Book edition, 1965), p. 449.
17. Suzanne Chevalier-Skolnikoff, "Homosexual Behavior in a Laboratory Group of Stumptail Monkeys *(Macaca arctoides):* Forms, Contexts, and Possible Social Functions," *Archives of Sexual Behavior* 5 (November, 1976): 511–27.
18. Reported by Dr. Paul Gebhard during his lecture on "Mammalian Sexual Behavior," Summer Program, Institute for Sex Research, Indiana University, July 20, 1977.
19. James Graham-Murray, *A History of Morals* (London: Library 33 Limited, 1966), pp. 64–66.
20. Polybius, *The Histories*, trans. Mortimer Chambers (New York: Washington Square Press, 1966), p. 306.
21. McNeill, p. 53.
22. Petronius, *The Satyricon*, trans. William Arrowsmith (New York: New American Library, Mentor Books, 1959), pp. 90–92.
23. Suetonius, *The Twelve Caesars*, trans. Robert Graves (Middlesex, England: Penguin Books, 1957), p. 223.
24. McNeill, p. 52.
25. Enslin, p. 147.
26. John Milton, *Paradise Lost*, bk. 11, lines 632–34 and their context; see also *Paradise Regained*, bk. 2, lines 220–30.
27. *The Compact Edition of the Oxford English Dictionary*, S. V. "effeminate."
28. J. Rinzema, *The Sexual Revolution: Challenge and Response*, trans. Lewis B. Smedes (Grand Rapids, Mich.: Eerdmans, 1974), p. 105.

6. WHAT DOES SCIENCE SAY?

1. Evelyn Hooker, "Homosexuality," in *International Encyclopedia of the Social Sciences*, ed. David L. Sills (New York: Crowell, Collier, and Macmillan, 1968), 14: 222–33. Reprinted in *National Institute of Mental Health Task Force on Homosexuality: Final Report and Background Papers*, ed. John Livingood (Rockville, Md.: National Institute of Mental Health, 1972), pp. 11–21. This report will hereafter be referred to as *NIMH Report*.
2. Paul H. Gebhard, "Incidence of Overt Homosexuality in the United States and Western Europe," in *NIMH Report*, pp. 22–29.

3. Gebhard, p. 26; also see Alfred Kinsey et al., *Sexual Behavior in the Human Female* (Philadelphia: W. B. Saunders Co., 1953), repr. in (New York: Pocket Books, 1965), p. 469–72 (paperback).
4. Gebhard, pp. 27–28.
5. Ibid., p. 26.
6. Alan Bell, "The Homosexual as Patient," in *Sex Research Studies from the Kinsey Institute*, ed. Martin S. Weinberg (New York: Oxford University Press, 1976), p. 203.
7. Gebhard, pp. 27–28; Bell, p. 203; R. W. Ramsay, P. M. Heringa, and I. Boorsma, "A Case Study: Homosexuality in the Netherlands," in *Understanding Homosexuality: Its Biological and Psychological Bases*, ed. J. A. Loraine (New York: American Elsevier, 1974), p. 136.
8. *Towards a Quaker View of Sex*, rev. ed. (London: Friends Home Service Committee, 1964), p. 26.
9. Ramsay, Heringa, and Boorsma, p. 132.
10. John Money, "Statement on Antidiscrimination Regarding Sexual Orientation," *SIECUS Report* 6 (September, 1977): 3. The routine practice of forcing left-handed persons to switch to their right hands still goes on in some European countries. Likewise, a certain amount of discrimination against left-handed persons exists in the United States as well—a situation which spawned the formation of a Topeka, Kansas based organization called Lefthanders International. See Barbara Palmer, "Left Out: Post Office May Fire Banfield because He Works Left Handed," *Washington Star*, syndicated, as reprinted in Bloomington (Ind.) *Herald-Telephone*, June 3, 1977, p. 13.
11. Wilhelm Stekel, *The Homosexual Neurosis* (New York: Emerson Books, 1949), pp. 290–91.
12. Martin S. Weinberg and Colin J. Williams, *Male Homosexuals: Their Problems and Adaptations* (New York: Oxford University Press, 1974). Quoted from Penguin Books edition, pp. 17–19.
13. David Lester, *Unusual Sexual Behavior: The Standard Deviations* (Springfield, Ill.: Charles C. Thomas, Publisher, 1975), pp. 71–72.
14. George W. Brown, *Sociological Research—How Seriously Do We Take It?* (London: Bedford College, University of London, 1974), p. 10.
15. Paul Chance, "Facts that Liberated the Gay Community" (An interview with Evelyn Hooker), *Psychology Today* 9 (December, 1975): 52–55, 101; see also Martin Hoffman, "Homosexuality," *Today's Education* (November, 1970), as reprinted in *Focus: Human Sexuality* (Sluice Dock, Guilford, Ct.: The Dushkin Publishing Group Annual Editions, 1976), pp. 196–98.
16. Paul Gebhard, "Human Sexual Research and Its Impact on Values," lecture presented at the Ad Hoc Committee for Humanistic Affairs Forum, Indiana University, Bloomington, Indiana, March 12, 1977. Also see *NIMH Report*.
17. For a discussion of the term *healthy homosexual*, see George Weinberg, *Society and the Healthy Homosexual* (New York: Doubleday Anchor Books, 1973).
18. News Release, The American Psychiatric Association, Washington, D. C., December 15, 1973.

19. Gebhard, 1977 lecture.
20. Andrea Kincses Oberstone and Harriet Sukoneck, "Psychological Adjustment and Style of Life of Single Lesbians and Single Heterosexual Women" (Paper presented at the Western Psychological Association Convention, Sacramento, California, April, 1975); Thomas R. Clark, "Homosexuality as a Criterion Predictor of Psychopathology in Non-Patient Males" (Paper presented at the Western Psychological Association Convention, April, 1975); Henry Heald and Mary Finley, "Alienation and Sexuality: a Comparison of Homosexual and Heterosexual Women" (Paper read at the annual meeting of the American Sociological Association, San Francisco, California, 1975). For a summary of studies before 1975, see Weinberg and Williams, pp. 446–47, n. 5.
21. Weinberg and Williams, especially the Preface and chapters 1, 11, and 22.
22. Michael Schofield, *Sociological Aspects of Homosexuality* (Boston: Little Brown and Co., 1965), as summarized in Hooker, *NIMH Report*, p. 18.

7. FROM HOMOPHOBIA TO UNDERSTANDING

1. George Weinberg, *Society and the Healthy Homosexual* (Garden City, New York: Doubleday Anchor Books, 1973), chap. 1.
2. Bloomington (Indiana) *Daily Herald-Telephone*, April 13, 1977.
3. Weinberg, chapter 1.
4. Jeremy Seabrook, *A Lasting Relationship* (London: Allen Lane, 1976), pp. 231, 17.
5. Summary of a statement by Paul Gebhard in discussion of a paper presented by Alan Bell, "Research in Homosexuality: Back to the Drawing Board," as part of a conference on sex research held at the State University of New York at Stony Brook, June 5–9, 1974. Reprinted in *Archives of Sexual Behavior* 4 (July, 1975): 431.
6. C. A. Tripp, *The Homosexual Matrix* (New York: McGraw-Hill, 1975), pp. 209–12.
7. Richard Green, *Sexual Identity Conflict in Children and Adults* (New York: Basic Books, 1974), p. 74.
8. Hooker, *NIMH Report*, p. 11 (see note 1, chapter 6 for full reference).
9. William Fitch, *Christian Perspectives on Sex and Marriage* (Grand Rapids, Mich.: Eerdmans, 1971), p. 133.
10. Paul D. Meier, *Christian Child-Rearing and Personality Development* (Grand Rapids, Mich.: Baker Book House, 1977), p. 52.
11. Berkeley Rice, "Coming of Age in Sodom and New Milford," *Psychology Today* 9 (September, 1975): 64–66.
12. Meier, pp. 52–53.
13. Richard Green, "Atypical Sex Role Development in Children" (Lecture presented at the Institute for Sex Research Summer Program, Indiana University, Bloomington, Indiana, July 26, 1976.) Also see Green, *Sexual Identity Conflict*.
14. In her current research on matched samples of female transsexuals (women who want to become men) and lesbians, Dr. Anke Ehrhardt found that the transsexuals had fantasies that they were males while having sex relations with other women. This was not true of the lesbians. Reported by Dr. Ehrhardt at the Institute for Sex Research

Summer Program, Bloomington, Indiana, July 28, 1977. For further information on transsexualism, see Richard Green, *Sexual Identity Conflict;* Deborah Heller Feinbloom, *Transvestites and Transsexuals* (New York: Dial Press/Delacorte Press, 1976); and Thomas Kando, *Sex Change: The Achievement of Gender Identity among Feminized Transsexuals* (Springfield, Ill.: Charles C. Thomas, Publisher, 1973).

15. William Shakespeare, Sonnet 116. Emphasis added.

16. Robert Brain, *Friends and Lovers* (London: Hart-Davis, MacGibbon, 1976), pp. 223, 259–60.

17. For further discussion of this topic see Letha Scanzoni, "On Friendship and Homosexuality," *Christianity Today* 18 (September 27, 1974): 11–16; also Corbin Carnell, "Open and Shut Friendships," *Eternity* 28 (April, 1977): 22–24.

18. Alfred Kinsey et al., *Sexual Behavior in the Human Female* (Philadelphia: W. B. Saunders Co., 1953; repr. in (New York: Pocket Books, 1965), p. 475 (paperback).

19. Statement made by Anita Bryant on "Donahue," syndicated television program, April 13, 1977. Also see Frank Rose, "Trouble in Paradise," *New Times* 8 (April 15, 1977): 44–53.

20. John Money and Anke Ehrhardt, *Man and Woman, Boy and Girl* (Baltimore: Johns Hopkins University Press, 1972), chap. 11; see also Green, *Sexual Identity Conflict;* and Hooker in *NIMH Report.*

21. Mary Calderone, "Of Dade County, Homosexuals, and Rights," *SIECUS Report* 6 (September, 1977):2.

22. Alan Bell, discussion following a paper, "The Appraisal of Homosexuality," presented at the Summer Program in Human Sexuality, Institute for Sex Research, Indiana University, Bloomington, Indiana, July 23, 1976.

23. William Simon and John Gagnon, "The Lesbians: A Preliminary Overview," in *Sexual Deviance*, ed. John Gagnon and William Simon (New York: Harper & Row, 1967), p. 255.

24. Parker Rossman, "The Pederasts," *Transaction/Society* 10 (March-April, 1973). Reprinted in Erich Goode and Richard Troiden, eds., *Sexual Deviance and Sexual Deviants* (New York: William Morrow, 1974), pp. 396–409.

25. Roger H. Ard, "Why the Conservatives Won in Miami," *The Christian Century* 94 (August 3–10, 1977), p. 678.

26. As reported in the *New York Times*, July 17, 1977, p. 34. For a detailed report on this survey, see the special issue, "Homoisexuals in America," *The Gallup Opinion Index* 147 (October, 1977). Among other interesting findings were those related to religion and homosexuality. The Gallup researchers comment that "ironically, one of the key reasons why the lot of the homosexual in the United States is a difficult one is that Americans are, at least outwardly, a highly religious people. In their views toward homosexuals, churchgoers and church members are far more inclined to take a negative stance than are non-churchgoers and people who are not members of a church." Among persons who believe homosexuals can be good Christians or good Jews, 74 percent favor equal employment rights for gays, whereas only 34 percent of persons who do *not* believe homosexuals can be good Christians or good Jews are in favor of such rights. According to the researchers, "this same pattern of opinion

also obtains on the other questions in the survey—whether gays should be hired for specific occupations, whether homosexual relations between consenting adults should be legalized, and whether gays should be allowed to adopt children. These differences are among the most dramatic found in the survey"(p. 21).

27. Personal interview. See Letha Scanzoni, "Conservative Christians and Gay Civil Rights," *The Christian Century* 93 (October 13, 1976), p. 860.

28. This material was reported in a lecture entitled "Gender Development, Homosexuality, and Transsexualism," presented by Dr. Ehrhardt at the summer program of the Institute for Sex Research, Indiana University, Bloomington, Indiana, July 28, 1977. The findings will also be reported in the *Journal of Homosexuality*. See also Money and Ehrhardt.

29. Richard Green, during a lecture entitled "Atypical Sex Role Development in Children" presented at the summer program of the Institute for Sex Research, Indiana University, July 28, 1977. This data will be reported in full in a forthcoming issue of the *American Journal of Psychiatry*.

30. Ibid.

31. "Sex Hormones and Male Homosexuality in Comparative Perspective," *Archives of Sexual Behavior* 6, no. 4 (July, 1977): 297–321.

32. "Miami Acts Tuesday on Homosexual Bias," *New York Times*, June 5, 1977, p. 22.

33. "Sunday Observer: Role Models," *New York Times Magazine*, June 26, 1977, p. 10.

34. Earl V. Pullias and James D. Young, "A Model: An Example," in *A Teacher Is Many Things* (Bloomington: Indiana University Press, 1968), pp. 72–73.

35. *Compassion and Self-Hate: An Alternative to Despair* (New York: Ballantine Books, 1975), p. 5.

36. George Weinberg, chap. 4.

37. Hooker, *NIMH Report*, pp. 19–20; Maurice Leznoff and William Westley, "The Homosexual Community," *Social Problems* 3 (April, 1957):257–63; Evelyn Hooker, "The Homosexual Community," *Perspectives in Psychopathology* (New York: Oxford University Press, 1965), reprinted in Gagnon and Simon, eds., 1967, pp. 167–84.

38. Laud Humphreys, *Tearoom Trade: Impersonal Sex in Public Places* (Chicago, Aldine, 1970).

39. Letter to the Bloomington (Indiana) *Daily Herald-Telephone*, February 8, 1977.

40. Dennis Altman, *Homosexual Oppression and Liberation* (New York: Outerbridge and Lazard, 1971). Quoted from Discus/Avon Books edition, p. 66 (paperback).

41. Alan Bell, "The Appraisal of Homosexuality," p. 23.

42. Alan Bell, "The Homosexual as Patient," in *Human Sexuality: A Health Practitioner's Text*, ed. Richard Green (Williams and Wilkins Co., 1975), as reprinted in *Sex Research: Studies from the Kinsey Institute*, ed. Martin S. Weinberg (New York: Oxford University Press, 1976), p. 208. On the basis of his studies in West Germany, sociologist Siegrid Schafer suggests that while homosexual women "have internalized the sociosexual norms of combining love and sexuality equally as much as heterosexual women," with the result that lesbian partners tend to reinforce these norms in one another, males (both homosexual and heterosexual) have been socialized to view sex quite differently. "Males learn from the beginning of puberty, or even earlier, to

conceive of sexuality in and of itself," he explains. Among heterosexual men, tendencies to detach sex from the context of love and emotional involvement are restrained through the influence of their female partners and the institutions of marriage and family. "These inhibiting conditions do not exist among homosexual males," Schafer points out, adding that the situation is compounded by the standards of the male homosexual subculture where "sexual success is an important status symbol." See Siegrid Schafer, "Sociosexual Behavior in Male and Female Homosexuals: A Study in Sex Differences," *Archives of Sexual Behavior* 6 (September, 1977): 360–62.

43. Evelyn Hooker, *NIMH Report*, p. 19; see also Nancy Achilles, "The Development of the Homosexual Bar as an Institution," in Gagnon and Simon, eds., pp. 228–44; Richard Troiden, "Homosexual Encounters in a Highway Rest Stop," in Goode and Troiden, pp. 211–28; Humphreys; Martin S. Weinberg and Colin J. Williams, "Gay Baths and the Social Organization of Impersonal Sex," *Social Problems* 23 (December, 1975): 124–36.

44. Hooker, *NIMH Report*, and Hooker, "The Homosexual Community." See also the section on "Gay Marriage" in Letha and John Scanzoni, *Men, Women, and Change* (New York: McGraw-Hill, 1976), pp. 185–94.

45. Personal interview.

46. Tim and Beverly LaHaye, *The Act of Marriage* (Grand Rapids, Mich.: Zondervan, 1976), p. 264.

47. Carl F. H. Henry, "In and Out of the Gay World," in *Is Gay Good?*, ed. W. Dwight Oberholtzer (Philadelphia: Westminster Press, 1971), pp. 111–12.

8. THE DEBATE IN AMERICAN CHRISTENDOM

1. Howard Brown, *Familiar Faces, Hidden Lives* (New York: Harcourt Brace Jovanovich, 1976), pp. 89–95.

2. Brown, p. 81.

3. Sylvia Rudolph, "One of Our Family Is Gay," *The Christian Home* 9 (May, 1977): 16–18.

4. Lewis Penhall Bird, "Deviance vs. Variance in Sexual Behavior," *Christian Medical Society Journal* 6 (Summer, 1975): 9–17.

5. Ed Wheat, *Sex Problems and Sex Techniques in Marriage* (Springdale, Arkansas: Bible Believers Cassettes, 1975), cassette no. 2, side 1.

6. Herbert J. Miles, *Sexual Happiness in Marriage* (Grand Rapids, Mich.: Zondervan, 1967), p. 81.

7. Tim and Beverly LaHaye, *The Act of Marriage* (Grand Rapids, Mich.: Zondervan, 1976), p. 275.

8. H. L. Ellison, *Ezekiel: The Man and His Message* (Grand Rapids, Mich.: Eerdmans, 1956), p. 89. See also Ezek. 18:5-13.

9. Brochure published by Evangelicals Concerned, c/o Dr. Ralph Blair, 30 East 60th Street, New York, New York 10022.

10. Maurice R. Irvin, "What the Bible Says About Sex," *Alliance Witness* 110 (July 16,

1975), p. 5. Also see Dennis F. Kinlaw, "A Biblical View of Homosexuality," in *The Secrets of Our Sexuality*, ed. Gary R. Collins (Waco: Word, 1976), pp. 104–15.

11. Ralph Blair, *An Evangelical Look at Homosexuality*, rev. ed. (New York: Evangelicals Concerned, 1977), p. 15.

12. Troy Perry is pastor and founder of the Metropolitan Community Church (MCC), a denomination which welcomes homosexuals and provides one of the few public places where they can meet in a social and spiritual atmosphere instead of in the more specifically sexual atmosphere of the bars or baths. Founded in 1968 in Los Angeles, the MCC now has more than forty churches which offer their congregations not only worship services and Bible studies but also discussion groups, fellowship hours, covered-dish dinners, and even holiday dinners for those whose families are far away. In his homespun autobiography, Troy Perry explains that he does not believe there should be a segregated church for homosexuals, but that anti-gay discrimination practiced by the churches of the United States forced him to found the MCC. It was founded, he says, so that "gays would have a place to worship God in dignity, and not as lepers and outcasts, but as His creation, as His children." See Troy Perry, *The Lord Is My Shepherd and He Knows I'm Gay* (Los Angeles: Nash Publishing, 1972), pp. 221–22.

13. "PUBC Position Paper on Homosexuality," *The Presbyterian Layman* 10 (April, 1977), p. 2.

14. "Affirmation on the Family," issued by the Continental Congress on the Family, Post Office Box 14249, Omaha, Nebraska 68114, 1975.

15. Joseph Bayly, "The Bible and Two Tough Topics," *Eternity* 25 (August, 1974): 41–42.

16. Margaret Evening, *Who Walk Alone* (Downers Grove, Ill.: InterVarsity Press, 1974), p. 62.

17. Mary Clark, "On Drawing Lines" (Unpublished paper, 1977).

18. Darrell J. Doughty, "Homosexuality and Obedience to the Gospel" (Paper delivered at the hearings of the Special Task Force to Study the Issue of the Ordination of an Avowed Homosexual, Presbytery of New York City, March, 1977). This paper is included in a special packet on ordination of homosexuals available for $3.00 from the Task Force to Study Homosexuality, The United Presbyterian Church of the U. S. A., 475 Riverside Drive, Room 1020, New York, New York 10027.

19. John E. Wagner, "Psychological Studies: From Gothard to Gay," *Christianity Today* 19 (May 9, 1975): 811.

9. PROPOSING A HOMOSEXUAL CHRISTIAN ETHIC

1. Lewis B. Smedes, *Sex for Christians* (Grand Rapids, Mich.: Eerdmans, 1976). See especially pp. 70–73.

2. Norman Pittenger, *Time for Consent: A Christian's Approach to Homosexuality* (London: SCM Press, 1970), pp. 116–17. See also John McNeill, *The Church and the Homosexual* (Kansas City: Sheed Andrews & McMeel, 1976), pp. 160–64.

3. Helmut Thielicke, "The Problem of Homosexuality," in *The Ethics of Sex*, trans.

John W. Doberstein (New York: Harper & Row, 1964). Quoted from Baker Book House edition, pp. 269–92 (paperback).

4. J. Rinzema, *The Sexual Revolution* (Grand Rapids, Mich.: Eerdmans, 1974), p. 106.

5. R. W. Ramsay, P. M. Heringa, and I. Boorsma, "A Case Study: Homosexuality in the Netherlands," in *Understanding Homosexuality: Its Biological and Psychological Bases* (New York: American Elsevier, 1974), pp. 121–39.

6. Ibid., p. 128.

7. Alex Davidson, *The Returns of Love* (Downers Grove, Ill.: InterVarsity Press, 1970).

8. Daniel C. Maguire, "The Vatican on Sex," *Commonweal* 103 (February 27, 1976): 138–39.

9. David A. Fraser, "Sensuous Theology," *Reformed Journal* 27 (February, 1977): 24.

10. Theodore W. Jennings, "Homosexuality and the Christian Faith," *Christian Century* 94 (February 16, 1977): 138.

11. Rosemary R. Ruether, "The Personalization of Sexuality," in *From Machismo to Mutuality*, ed. Rosemary R. Ruether and Eugene C. Bianchi (New York: Paulist Press, 1976), p. 83.

12. McNeill, pp. 32, 194.

13. James Nelson, "Homosexuality and the Church," *Christianity and Crisis* 37 (April 4, 1977), 63–69.

14. Ramsay, Heringa, and Boorsma, p. 126.

15. Walter Barnett, *Sexual Freedom and the Constitution* (Alburquerque: University of New Mexico Press, 1973), p. 11.

16. Erving Goffman, *Stigma* (Englewood Cliffs: Prentice-Hall, 1963), p. 30.

17. McNeill, pp. 155–56. McNeill himself has been experiencing the "social and psychological stigma" he writes about. Within a year of the August, 1976 publication of his book, a directive from the Vatican's Sacred Congregation of the Faith had ordered him to cease lecturing on the topic of homosexuality or any other area of sex ethics. Furthermore, future editions of *The Church and the Homosexual* may not carry the *imprimi potest* (a notation of the Roman Catholic Church's permission to print a book as worthy of discussion even though the views set forth may not be those officially endorsed by the church). See "Jesuit Theologian Silenced," *Christian Century* 94 (September 21, 1977): 809.

18. *Huck Finn and His Critics*, ed. Richard Lettis, et al. (New York: Macmillan, 1962), p. 187.

19. Paul Oestreicher, B.B.C.'s "Thought for the Day" broadcasts, May 17–20, 1976. Reprinted as "Aspects of Freedom" in *Christian* (Annunciation 1977): 188. This entire issue of *Christian* is devoted to discussions of homosexuality from a Christian perspective. Available from the Institute of Christian Studies, 7 Margaret Street, London W. 1., England.

Recommended for Further Reading

I F WE hope to reach out in Christian love to our neighbor, the homosexual, it is important that we inform ourselves on the subject. Below is a selected list of books that may be helpful. Other helpful books and articles are discussed in the text and cited in the Notes.

FOR GENERAL INFORMATION

Bell, Alan P. *Homosexuality.* SIECUS Study Guide, no. 2. rev. ed. New York: Sex Information and Education Council of the U.S., 1976. Distributed by Behavioral Publications.

A concise sixteen-page overview of present scientific knowledge and theory concerning homosexuality, written by a leading research psychologist in the field of human sexuality.

Livingood, John M., ed. *National Institute of Mental Health Task Force on Homosexuality: Final Report and Background Papers.* Rockville, Md.: National Institute of Mental Health, DHEW publication number (HSM) 72–9116, 1972. (Available from Supt. of Documents, U.S. Government Printing Office, Washington, D.C. 20402.)

A collection of specially prepared papers by scholars in different academic disciplines which offers a variety of perspectives on homosexuality.

Martin, Del and Phyllis Lyon. *Lesbian/Woman.* New York: Bantam Books, 1972.

Written by two women who have lived for many years in a committed lesbian relationship, this book presents a non-sensational, honest "view from the inside" describing the daily lives and struggles (including religious struggles) of homosexual women.

Silverstein, Charles. *A Family Matter: A Parents' Guide to Homosexuality.* New York: McGraw-Hill Book Company, 1977.

> *Vitally important reading for the parents and families of homosexuals and for pastors and anyone involved in homosexual counseling. No one should recommend that homosexuals should seek medical, religious, or psychological cures without reading Silverstein's carefully researched parallels between nineteenth-century "cures" for female sexual desire and twentieth-century "cures" for homosexuality. The book is marred only by Dr. Silverstein's assumption that all homosexuals should reveal their sexual orientation to their families in order to avoid "lying and deception." Unfortunately, the truth is more complex than that: some families send out clear signals that they do not want to know the truth about the homosexual in their midst, and their signals should probably be respected.*

Weinberg, George. *Society and the Healthy Homosexual.* Garden City, New York: Doubleday Anchor Books, 1973.

> *An illuminating discussion of homophobia, the injustices involved in trying to change homosexuals into heterosexuals, homosexual self-acceptance, and communication with parents of homosexuals.*

Weinberg, Martin S. and Colin J. Williams. *Male Homosexuals: Their Problems and Adaptations.* New York: Oxford University Press, 1974. (Also available as a Penguin paperback.)

> *Written by two American sociologists, this book presents a comparative study of more than two thousand homosexual men in three societies: the United States, the Netherlands, and Denmark. Sections on "Religious Background" and "Religiosity" are included.*

MATERIALS SPECIFICALLY DEALING WITH RELIGION AND HOMOSEXUALITY

Bailey, Derrick Sherwin. *Homosexuality and the Western Christian Tradition.* London: Longmans, Green & Co., 1955. Reprint. Hamden, Conn.: Shoestring Press, Archon Books, 1975.

> *A pioneering study of homosexuality against a background of biblical interpretation, theology, and church history.*

Blair, Ralph. *An Evangelical Look At Homosexuality.* rev. ed., New York: HCC, Inc., 1977. (Available from Evangelicals Concerned, c/o Dr. Ralph Blair, 30 East 60th Street, New York, New York 10022.)

> *Addressed primarily to homosexual Christians and written by the head of the Homosexual Community Counseling Center and editor of the* Homosexual Counseling Journal, *this pamphlet frankly examines both evangelical attitudes and the message of the Bible concerning homosexuality.*

Christianity and Crisis (May 30–June 13, 1977). (Available for $1.20 per copy from *Christianity and Crisis*, 537 West 121st Street, New York, New York 10027.) A special combined issue on homosexuality. See also the companion piece by James B. Nelson, "Homosexuality and the Church," in the April 4, 1977 issue (vol. 37).

Rational and responsible Christians wrestling with the difficult issues concerning homosexual Christians.

Davidson, Alex. *The Returns of Love: A Contemporary Christian View of Homosexuality.* Downers Grove, Ill.: InterVarsity Press, 1970.

Through a series of letters, a young man shares with a friend his agonies and struggles as a homosexual Christian who yearns for same-sex love and sexual expression but is persuaded that, for a Christian, the only answer is control and celibacy.

Jones, Clinton R. *Homosexuality and Counseling.* Philadelphia: Fortress Press, 1974.

An Episcopal priest who specializes in counseling offers excellent advice on how to help homosexual persons "out of pain and toward fulfillment" as self-accepting and responsible persons. Vital reading for pastors and counselors. The many stories of homosexual-related problems and solutions should also provide enlightenment for almost any reader.

McNeill, John. *The Church and the Homosexual.* Kansas City: Sheed, Andrews, & McMeel, 1976.

Written by a Jesuit priest and self-identified homosexual celibate, this profoundly Christian study includes thoughtful discussion of the scriptural handling of homosexuality and suggestions about the positive contributions of homosexuals to the life of the church.

Oraison, Marc. *The Homosexual Question: An Attempt to Understand an Issue of Increasing Urgency Within a Christian Perspective.* New York: Harper & Row, 1977.

Although limited by its author's Freudian assumptions about homosexuality as a simple matter of arrested emotional development and by the narrowness of his sampling of homosexual persons (his remarks are based only on people he has met in his roles of priest and psychoanalyst), this book is valuable for its demonstration of the complexities and the involuntary nature of the homosexual orientation.

Pittenger, Norman. *Time for Consent: A Christian's Approach to Homosexuality.* rev. ed. London: SCM Press, 1970.

A noted Anglican theologian struggles with theological and ethical aspects of the homosexual question and concludes with a "plea for Christian openness to the homosexual and a plea to the homosexual, whether male or female, to believe that there is a place for him in the Christian fellowship."

Rinzema, J. *The Sexual Revolution: Challenge and Response*. Translated by Lewis B. Smedes. Grand Rapids, Mich.: Eerdmans, 1974.

Rinzema's few pages concerning homosexuality are compassionate, insightful, and challenging, and they are written with a profound respect for the authority of Scripture.

Thielicke, Helmut. *The Ethics of Sex*. Translated by John W. Doberstein. Grand Rapids, Mich.: Baker Book House, 1975.

A renowned evangelical theologian compassionately explores the ethical options for an "incurable" predisposition to homosexuality which must be accepted as a "divine dispensation." First published in America in 1964, this book is important as one of the earliest breakthroughs of evangelical thinking on this topic.

Woods, Richard. *Another Kind of Love: Homosexuality and Spirituality*. Chicago: Thomas More Press, 1977.

Addressed primarily to homosexual persons and secondarily to all who care about them, this book by a Dominican priest is upbeat, well informed, and full of honest confrontation with the positive and negative aspects of being both homosexual and Christian. Woods gives direct and helpful advice concerning celibacy, chastity, pornography, modesty of clothing, gay bars and baths, and the pressing task of gay Christians to "redeem the gay community."

Index of Names and Subjects

Index of Scripture References